Physical Factors in Growth and Development
Joseph Di Leo

Coping With the Unseen Environment:
an Introduction to the Vocational
Rehabilitation of Blind Persons
Herbert Rusalem

The Forecast of Fulfillment
Henry V. Cobb

Right to Education
Leopold Lippman and I. Ignacy Goldberg

Helping Every Trainable Mentally Retarded Child

BERNICE B. BAUMGARTNER

TEACHERS COLLEGE PRESS
Teachers College, Columbia University
New York and London

Baumgartner, Bernice B.
    Helping every trainable mentally retarded child.

    (Teachers College series in special education)
    Published in 1960 under title: Helping the
    trainable mentally retarded child.
    Bibliography: p.
    1. Mentally handicapped children—Education.
I. Title. [DNLM: 1. Education of mentally re-
tarded. LC4602 B348h]
LC4601.B35 1975   371.9'283   75-2494
ISBN 0-8077-2472-6

Manufactured in the United States of America

Foreword

Helping Every Trainable Mentally Retarded Child is not the usual updating of an earlier publication. The inclusion of the word "Every" in the title broadens the readers' perspective and is a reflection of a strongly developing concern for the vast numbers of children who, because of severe developmental defect or delay, have been denied their chance for an education.

Bernice Baumgartner, a master teacher, is an active and vocal advocate of public school attendance by children often deemed too handicapped for inclusion in the usual community programs. Commitment to the handicapped has changed since 1960 when this volume's predecessor, *Helping the Trainable Mentally Retarded Child*, appeared. It was then one of the few clear descriptions of programs designed to educate the target group of children, those about whom public controversy raged. Debates, public and private, focused on whether "trainable retarded" children were to be public education's responsibility — or whether children incapable of "contributing to society" as adults were entitled to the support of public education. Miss Baumgartner clearly expressed in her monograph the conviction that the children not only had a place in the educational system, but could all learn. She, on the basis of her leadership as an educator in residential institutions and in the community centers established by groups of parents, prepared the earlier program statement. For over a decade, the document served as a guide for program development throughout the nation.

In updating *Helping the Trainable Mentally Retarded Child*, Miss Baumgartner has clearly expanded the target population; her approach is consistent with the nation's renewed and vital efforts on behalf of all children. The material in the present book is designed to share some fundamental experience in fostering the learning of boys and girls who in the 1960's and even in the '70's were considered to be too low-functioning to warrant public instruction. The massive litigations over the *Right to Education* as discussed by Lippman and Goldberg call for school action, for example, in locating all of the children in the Commonwealth of Pennsylvania, in assessing their educational needs, and in providing a program to meet those needs. Miss Baumgartner has addressed this challenge. Her respect for all children is inherent in this realistic charting of a movement as yet barely acknowledged but strongly felt. The importance of the retarded individual and of his or her family are the alpha and omega of the program base proposed here. Recognition of the management problems being encountered by school personnel and families is evident in the direct approach to individualization of instruction, especially in the face of the unique complexities presented by each child.

This book is written for the practitioner by a practitioner who has lived and worked through the organizational, administrative, and pragmatic situations she has described. The suggestions she has included in this guide will encourage teachers, administrators, and parents in their efforts to assume responsibility for the education of their children who are new to the schools. The principle underlying this book is that all children can learn and that educators have a major role in facilitating the learning of the multiply and seriously handicapped child.

Frances P. Connor
Chairman, Department of Special Education
Teachers College, Columbia University

Author's Preface

This is a grass-roots publication made possible by the work of special educators and parents from the early 1950's to the present in helping educate thousands of mentally retarded children throughout the United States. Such education is possible because of legislation that began by mandating public school classes for the trainable mentally retarded children in the 1950's and continued through the court orders and legislation mandating education for all children, including the severely and profoundly mentally retarded, in the 1970s (18).*

This publication reflects early efforts to develop programs to meet the individual needs of trainable mentally retarded children. For instance, in 1953 a project was developed by the Illinois State Department of Education and the University of Illinois to find out what could be accomplished for trainable mentally retarded children in the public schools. From this project came our first *Curriculum Guide for Trainable Mentally Handicapped Children* in 1955. This guide helped teachers plan programs as legislation came into being in many states.

In 1960 the publication *Helping the Trainable Mentally Retarded Child* expanded the growing knowledge of proven methods of helping the trainable mentally retarded child in the public schools. The book included methods being used in

*Numbers in parentheses refer to numbered items in the list of selected references in the back of this book.

reaching some of the children who were excluded from the public schools, who were being educated in private parent-operated classes and in some state schools and hospitals.

The present publication, *Helping Every Trainable Mentally Retarded Child*, retains the philosophy that "every child can learn" that was implied in the earlier publications. It expands that philosophy by discussing up-to-date techniques and methods being used by many teachers and supervisors involved in teaching the school-aged trainable mentally retarded child and the mentally retarded infant and toddler being helped in other facilities.

I have been fortunate to be in many situations throughout the country where action was bringing about the education of all children through the Right to Education (18). As In-service Training Advisor for the Right to Education for the Department of Education in Pennsylvania it was possible for me to draw upon the tremendous efforts of others, disseminate information, and assist in intermeshing workable ideas. Such responsibilities continue to be carried out through the Pennsylvania Association for Retarded Children and the in-service education program of the Pennsylvania Federation Council for Exceptional Children as we share this information.

Within a context of burgeoning ideas and budding research, new children are entering classes for the trainable mentally retarded. Teachers and parents appear to leave their fears and apprehensions behind and acquire ever-increasing expectations as they find that every child can learn. Many school people feel that each child entering a program for the trainable mentally retarded should be an integral part of that program. No child should be excluded from a program unless he is placed in a more adequate program for him in the public schools. This approach takes into account each child's uniqueness—his individual capabilities, weaknesses, and family background.

This handbook is intended to serve as a guide for such a program, suggesting individual approaches for different children. It is couched in language that will be intelligible to the children's parents, most of whom are laymen and therefore unfamiliar with technical educational terminology. An effort has been made to present practical suggestions for the teacher, particularly the teacher who is inexperienced in working with the lowest-functioning child. A check list for appraising program quality is included for administrators. It is earnestly hoped that the book will be used by educators and parents in a cooperative venture.

In working with administrators, teachers, parents' groups, college personnel, and classes for retarded children, I have been privileged to put into practice the theories discussed in this book, and I have witnessed fruitful results. I have seen many so-called "hopeless cases" develop into socially adjusted members of their homes and other environments. I have watched personalities emerge as children learned to care for themselves and be useful to others.

I sincerely believe that sensitive teachers and parents, by using an individual approach for each child, can help every trainable child—including the most severely and profoundly mentally retarded—develop unforeseen potentials. No child is without some capacity to learn.

B.B.B.

Contents

1

The Child Comes to School

The trainable mentally retarded child comes to school with his own capacity for growth in an education program. His development, like any child's, is the result of an integration of biology and culture, shaped by people and events. He is what he is because of a combination of factors—genes, prenatal and postnatal environments, and the ability to learn from experiences.

The term "trainable mentally retarded" (TMR) indicates that this child is functioning mentally at half or less than half his chronological age. He may be multiply handicapped and considered severely or profoundly mentally retarded. His language development and perceptual function are probably at about the same level as his mental age. The child's mental retardation may be the result of Down's syndrome, brain injury, epilepsy, cerebral palsy, or environmental deprivation, to mention only a few possible causes. In addition, the retardation may be complicated by physical handicaps such as spasticity or defective sight or hearing. Except for the clinical conditions (such as Down's syndrome, cretinism, and microcephaly), the retarded child is not very different from the average child in his physical appearance. His mental development, however, may differ from the normal in rate as well as in degree.

This child has the same deep-rooted need to be loved and wanted as does any other child. He needs a feeling of security. He needs to relate to other people and get along with them. He needs to be active and creative. As these needs are fulfilled and he becomes oriented to the world around him, the child manifests a knowledge of who he is and what he can do. Teachers should be constantly aware of these basic needs as they plan meaningful experiences for individuals as well as for the class as a whole. Parents too should be aware of these needs and of their relationship to the ongoing experiences of the child while he is at home.

To an extent varying with the individual, the TMR child is capable of growing in self-concept, motor and perceptual development, self-care, communication, social interaction, self-help, and independence. Just as with other children, patterns of behavior will evolve. The child will grow physically if he is given the proper food, become aggressive, hostile, or withdrawn if he is unable or not allowed to express himself. He will react to different people in different ways, and may attach strange and unrealistic meanings to experiences that are beyond his comprehension.

Some youngsters have little or no oral communication, and what little speech others use may be confined to single words or simple phrases. Some children may have no apparent interest in anything outside themselves and will play alone. Some may have objectionable habits, like screaming or upsetting furniture.

Early state regulations for admission to public school classes for the trainable mentally retarded required that the child be toilet trained, ambulatory, able to make his needs known, physically not a danger to himself or others, and able to profit from the program. The wording of these regulations eliminated many children from public schools who would have been able to grow if given the opportunity. Even private and state residential schools did not include children in their classes because they "could not profit," or because they were not toilet trained. Fortunately, a great many teachers and parents have become more realistic. They know that the behaviors of every child can be modified regardless of how the child is functioning. Even children called crib cases can change, grow, and remain in the community when someone takes the time to help them learn to help themselves in areas such as toilet training and eating. The multiply handicapped child with severe retardation can be taught through the use of equipment and instructional materials that meet his special requirements, and through the ability of the adult to work with him on the level at which he is functioning.

In answer to a questionnaire 80 teachers of TMR classes listed the personal mannerisms that characterized the behavior of the children they taught. With few exceptions, the replies referred to physical movement and sound production. The activities fell into four general classifications: simple movement of the child's own body, as in jumping, wiggling, rocking, or swinging arms or legs; movement from one part of the room to another; movement involving an object, as in throwing, pounding, or upsetting blocks; movement directed toward the child's own body, as in scratching, tearing clothes, or pulling hair. The child's need for movement is reflected in his efforts to release both physical and emotional tensions in bodily action. The two kinds of vocal production the teachers mentioned were self-produced sounds, such as screaming and gutteral noises, and verbal activities. Both indicate an effort to communicate; the sounds are the earlier stage and the verbal activity comes later.

When the child's efforts to communicate are not understood he becomes frustrated. Inability to express himself and be understood by others constitutes perhaps the strongest inhibiting force in the life of the trainable mentally retarded child. Consequently, communication with others becomes a prime objective in both home and school. Since the TMR child's behavior pattern seems to be divided between bodily movement and efforts to communicate, the problem for parents and teachers is to transmute the physical movement into communication.

Communication is the core of the educational program for the TMR child, for it unlocks the door to intellectual and emotional development. The TMR child is considered adjusted socially when he can get along with other people, understand himself, practice good work habits, follow directions, be well-groomed, be trusted, attain personal adequacy in self-care, and follow the rules of personal health and safety. But before he can achieve these goals, he must be able to communicate. Helping him communicate is the task of teachers and parents as the TMR child comes to school.

2

The Child Communicates

Social communication, as the term is used in this book, has a much broader meaning than simply the oral, gestured, or written message. It involves the ability to express inner feelings and thoughts and the comprehension of what is conveyed by the words or gestures of others. It constitutes the foundation of the TMR child's ability to develop personally, socially, and occupationally. It allows him to grow emotionally as he learns to understand. When such a child begins to communicate he first discovers himself. Then he gradually relates himself to other people. Later he uses his skills to help himself, and finally to help others.

Long before a child can speak he learns to express his feelings through bodily movement. Early expression takes the form of eye contact, then of following an adult with his eyes, babbling and screaming to get attention. Later he may nod or shake his head, grab an adult to command notice, jump up and down in joy or anger, or lead an adult to the object he wants. The child's actions constitute an effort to communicate. If he receives acceptance, encouragement, and guidance, these actions may grow into socially acceptable behavior. The sensitive adult is constantly alert for such movement, particularly its first appearance, considering it a clue to the level of development. Teachers and parents share understandings as the child achieves a readiness for each step in developing communication that is meaningful to him. The TMR child's first effort to point out the object he desires, to participate in parallel play with another child or in group play with his classmates, to speak a word, to indicate an awareness of something or somebody in the outside world— all should be reported between home and school, so that a closely knit program of education can be effected.

Behavior at home differs from behavior at school far more than either teachers or parents realize. This is illustrated by the responses of the parents of 60 TMR children to the question: "What personal mannerisms characterize the behavior of your child?" While a few of the answers dealt with various types of movement and the efforts to communicate, most of the parents stressed temper tantrums, stubbornness, and other antisocial behavior. The differences between conduct at home and at school clearly indicate that a child's family often unwittingly pressures him and expects the impossible, with resultant emotional outbursts. The teacher, for the most part, accepts the child as he is, recognizes his limitations and his needs, and tries to transmute his bodily movement and vocal efforts at communication into socially acceptable activities.

Teaching social behavior means following the pattern of moving from the familiar to the unknown, from large-muscle activity to smaller movements. For this reason it is particularly important for both teachers and parents to understand the different levels at which the child is functioning, so that they can guide him forward.

STAGES IN COMMUNICATION DEVELOPMENT

Research over a period of years has provided the teacher with a good concept of the sequential development of a child's communication. Developmental guidelines can indicate the level at which the child is functioning, but teachers should remember that every child will not necessarily pass through every stage in the sequence.

In general, the first stage of the development of communication is eye contact, after which the child learns to follow with his eyes and use gestures and physical action—grabbing and hitting people to get attention, using gestures but not words, using gesturing primarily, with some words, leading adults to what he wants, and pantomiming what he wants to say.

During the second stage, the child tries to use sounds to convey meaning—attempting to vocalize but with only air issuing from the larynx, vocalizing when excited, babbling, using the initial sound in a word, and making sounds during group activity.

In the third stage, the child imitates sounds, words, and actions—imitating the teacher during activity, imitating high and low tones in music, but not with words, imitating sounds of others, and repeating words on request but not in real situations.

During the fourth stage, the child attempts to verbalize meaningfully—using single words to include proper names, common exclamations and greetings, identifying objects and pictures with one word, using single words in communicative situations, and combining two or more words.

In the fifth stage of communication development, the child participates in a group—repeating all words in such group activities as finger plays, performing activities before a group, leading group activity, and participating in group discussion.

In the sixth stage of development, the child converses with others—speaking only when addressed, giving commands to others, asking questions, relating previous experiences, talking excessively on limited subjects, conversing with adults, conversing with peers, using polite language spontaneously, and taking the initiative in conversation.

Once the teacher and parents have a good idea of the stage of development in which the child is functioning, they can guide him toward the next stage. In doing this, they should constantly be aware of certain basic rules. They should keep the child occupied in activities where he can achieve success. These activities should alternate between strenuous and passive. Materials should be on the child's level of comprehension—simple, solid, familiar things—and be related to an unfamiliar concept or routine gradually, one step at a time.

Teachers and parents need self-discipline in this process. They should use positive encouraging statements and praise, avoiding arguments, threats, and anger, if possible. They should not equate work and punishment, or pressure the child beyond his capacities. If the child misbehaves violently, the teacher or parent should direct him toward some constructive activity.

DETECTING READINESS TO ADVANCE

Since the improvement in the child's developmental level plays such an important role in his further growth, parents and teachers should be constantly alert for clues that indicate an advance. Some clues derived from bodily movement are very simple. For example, Sharon, who had been spoon-fed all her life, was placed in a classroom for the trainable. One day she noticed the teacher drinking tea and excitedly gestured toward the cup. The teacher filled a cup with milk and gave it to Sharon, who picked it up and drank, unaided.

In another case, a group of youngsters visited a nearby classroom so their teacher might have a rest period. On their return, Jerry, who could not speak, placed his drawing near the blackboard and then opened the desk drawer where the masking tape was stored. The teacher, realizing that they had seen art work displayed on the walls of the other room, provided materials to enable all the children to exhibit their drawings. In another instance, a substitute teacher had to start the day without any briefing on the children. Only one child tried to communicate, so she took her beginning clue from him. He motioned to his socks and said "red," and to his shirt and said "blue." Some of the children in the classroom pointed to various articles of their clothing. The new teacher realized that they usually started the morning activities by discussing their clothes and their bodies. She began with an exercise of naming garments. When the children seemed restless she organized a game played in a circle: "Arms up, arms down, then we go round, round, round." The children could work off the tension of a new situation in physical activity while participating in a learning situation (i.e., identification of parts of the body).

Many of the clues are far more subtle, however, and require closer observation of a child's behavior in the classroom and his relationships with the other children. For example, Kathy stubbornly refused to enter the playground. Her teacher, rather than blame this on obstinacy, tried to understand her reasoning. In his report the teacher wrote: "I feel she was trying to find herself in the big vastness of it all. She felt insecure that there was nothing near to grab, to see. The space and emptiness made her feel insecure and she was afraid." The teacher did not force the child to go into the playground; instead he introduced her to rooms and spaces of increasing size. He arranged for her to be near a group of other children at all times. Whenever the class embarked on a new situation, the teacher was near enough to Kathy for her to take his hand if she wished to do so. He told her parents of the problem and of his approach to it; they gladly cooperated. One day, when the teacher felt Kathy was ready to come into a group, he played her favorite game on the edge of the playground. Kathy joined in the fun without hesitation.

ACTIVITIES THAT PROMOTE SELF-EXPRESSION

Dramatic play, through role-playing or puppetry, is a particularly effective tool for the child like Kathy who is withdrawn, shy, and fearful. Such children seem able to lose themselves in the realm of make-believe, finding security there that later carries over into the real world. When a child "becomes" Punchinello, or the zoo keeper, or Popeye, he creates a shield against the mortification he feels over his inability to express himself verbally. In one art period, the children made masks from paper bags and presented an impromptu play. Inarticulate Beth became so fond of hers that the teacher allowed her to keep it with her instead of storing it for future use. For days Beth role-played with the mask in front of her face whenever she attempted speech. Suddenly she no longer felt the need for the defense and stopped using the paper mask. In the words of her teacher, "She's not afraid of anything. She talks out and tells me what she wants. Before, I had to work hard to find out what she wanted; now she comes out and says that she wants to go to the park and feed the ducks."

Free play provides a child with one of the best means of self-expression available and should be carefully observed by the teacher for clues to the child's particular problems. Simply knowing that he can choose his own activities relaxes a tense child. For this reason many teachers plan a free play period at the beginning of the day, to allow the children to unwind after their trip to school. Some listen to music, singing along with it or keeping time by tapping feet or dancing, while others build with blocks, play with water, look at picture books, or pretend they are cooking and serving a meal. David, whose only sounds were "ma, da, wa," always ran to the telephone in his free play period, carrying on long and animated "conversations" with another child. Little Ingrid made believe she was washing and rocking a doll as she played with a pillow.

The skillful teacher realizes that no amount of talking or reading is as effective in teaching as is simply giving the child a chance to feel a tangible object or to participate in a situation for himself. Touching a table or watching rain spatter the window is infinitely more meaningful to the child than seeing a picture in a book or having an adult tell him about it. The teacher utilizes every situation in which the class expresses an interest to create a learning experience. For example, every morning as the school bus arrived at one school, a white-coated man in the doorway of the corner drugstore waved to the children. The teacher explained that this nice man was "our friend, the druggist," who was always ready to help when people got sick. Teacher and pupils walked to the corner to look at the store. The next day the druggist came to the class and shook their hands, asking them to come to the drugstore sometime for ice cream cones. The children played drugstore during their free play period and drew pictures of ice cream cones. They cut out a picture of a man in a white coat and taped it to the door. Finally one much-anticipated day the children went into the store for dessert after lunch. Fascinated, they watched the activities behind the soda fountain. As a cone was placed in one girl's hand she said, "I scree," her first attempt at oral communication.

Possibilities for field trips are limitless and provide incomparable opportunities for retarded children to learn to live in and with the community. They can make expeditions to parks, zoos, restaurants. They can watch street sweepers, mailmen, and policemen at work. By acting the part of the bus driver, by building a train station with blocks, by singing about the zoo animals, by drawing pictures of the farm he visited, a child can express himself. And in the process he is likely to grow up relaxed, secure, useful, and happy, able to communicate with other people in his own way.

3

All Children Can Learn

Most children can learn to communicate at some level. Many people who were unaware of this are now being led to awareness and acceptance of it as a result of Federal Court Orders, such as the "Right to Education" in Pennsylvania (18). Before the 1970's, educators were frequently convinced that a child should be declared uneducable if he were not toilet trained or could not feed himself. Such boundaries of educability existed only in the mind of a less enlightened society.

During the past 20 years I have observed changes in the attitudes of teachers who communicate with multiply handicapped children in day care centers and in public and private residential settings. Today, freed from the old negativism and stereotypes, teachers in public schools, too, are discovering within themselves unsuspected abilities to help every child make greater progress at each stage of his existence. More people are now convinced that every child has a potential, the limits of which are still unknown. Realization of this potential is highly dependent upon the teacher's ability to anticipate and analyze the difficulties, and to impart the skills essential to overcoming them.

This becomes an all-encompassing process. Ideally, it begins as soon as a child is identified as retarded in mental development, and continues within a span of experiences tailored to his needs and abilities. In accordance with this changing philosophy, special programs are now including infants and toddlers, three- and four-year-olds, and school-aged children from five to 21, with emphasis on the most severely and profoundly retarded.

INFANTS AND TODDLERS

Developmentally retarded children can learn in infancy and early childhood. Teachers and parents who are involved in programs for this age group no longer question this. For instance, eight such projects were undertaken in Pennsylvania,* under the Department of Public Welfare in 1971. The experiences that took place in these projects were the most exciting in many a year for everyone connected with them. Teachers began their observations by going into homes and learning from mothers and fathers. They found infants as young as two and three months establishing eye contact and making progress as they were stimulated and rewarded for their simple actions.

Where does education begin? There are many answers. As infants and young children lie on the floor and respond with a start to teacher or parent intervention, as they learn to move and feed themselves, they are becoming human beings in their own right. One excited parent called the school after the teacher's home visit to say, "You helped me find the answer. I just put my hand on top of Jimmy's hand and now he is spoon-feeding himself for the first time. I will bend his spoon as you suggested because he does have a hard time finding his mouth." The mother of a small undernourished child was concerned that her child took half an hour to drink his bottle of milk. By enlarging the holes in the nipple at the teacher's suggestion, she enabled the child to drink the milk more quickly and easily. Another child had trouble using a training cup. His teacher helped by simply removing the lid. A very young child does not eat. A teacher provides special exercises and stimulation to encourage the child to stay awake, so that when it is time to eat, he is hungry.

One supervisor gives this advice: "First and foremost, get

*Under Elementary and Secondary Education Act, Title I, P.L. 89-313.

the child's attention. Work from eye contact. No response? Keep at it with a smiling face and with a pleasant voice."

In one small residential setting, the coordinating teacher scheduled periods to work with toddlers from the time they awoke until they went to bed. For each of three daily shifts the staff included a teacher, teacher aides, and child care workers. Most of the children in the group were not toilet trained and no one had previously made an effort to teach them to feed themselves.

After a few months of training, one child who had rejected food and was not toilet trained learned to feed himself and was staying dry. Then he began to pull himself up and take a few steps. Teacher aides who previously had had a tendency to baby him because he was pleasant and lovable began to demand progress. Many children in this group slept and rejected food. They were supine and remained in cribs the greater part of the day. In three months, each member of this group was able to undress himself. All the children were wearing training pants and half were toilet trained. They spent a large part of the morning and afternoon on the floor, where they moved about, smiled at each other, touched each other, socialized, put together puzzles, worked with thick crayons, and even tried to change the records on the record player. In another setting the teacher's reports included these comments:

Mike progressed this week. We see little of his former screaming behavior. He lies still and seems to absorb what is going on around him. We will work with eye contact and encourage him to grasp objects. He seems to be especially happy in his bath and we find this a very good time to work with him.

Louis has fallen in love with his self-image! He mouths the mirror that is close to the floor. His previous self-destructive behavior has yet to be seen in the lab, and he allows a small smile to shine through every so often. He appears to dislike walking and prefers to be carried. We are working on words and self-help skills. When we find food reinforcement which is sufficiently nourishing to Louis, we may have more success with his walking.

Nathan has adapted very well to the lab. We were afraid that his being with younger children would disturb him, but on the contrary, he is now the "big cheese." He requires constant attention, although he is effective in coloring, pasting, finger painting and helping to take the other children, who are feeding themselves, to the dining room. We are helping him classify items, identify colors, and learn new words. When we get a sliding board and a record player, he will have more to challenge him.

Ned has progressed in several areas. He now participates in the self-feeding process, waving his spoon wildly while he eats with the other hand. He can drink his milk by himself. We follow him and join in his games. He will be able to walk soon as he is determined to get his balance. Social contact with adults seems to be a big reward factor to him which we will continue to use.

In another situation, 99 percent of the parents attend every parent-teacher meeting. Teachers working with public health nurses, in hospitals, and using interpreters when necessary involve many parents in disadvantaged areas.

The emotional climate in the various areas where teachers and parents work is unique. A parent enters a classroom with a spring in her step as she carries her three-month-old infant to the teacher, who is sitting on the floor near a large horizontal mirror placed low enough for the children to see themselves. Another parent cannot wait to tell the teacher that Johnny is moving on his own. The parents place the children on the floor and observe them with the teacher, watching for signals of "what comes next."

Parents of infants and toddlers who are helping to educate their children appear different from their counterparts who had to wait until children were five, six, or seven before receiving help, in the meantime being frustrated and allowing the child's abilities to be diminished.

Recently one special educator* said:

We are convinced such efforts will affect these children and their future education more than anything we have done in the last 20 years. We are convinced that many of these youngsters who would eventually be placed in sheltered workshops will not need to go to sheltered workshops. They will go into the mainstream of living just as any other children because we are reaching them

*John Lapidaikes, Executive Director, Lehigh Valley Association for Retarded Children, 1972.

at an early age. Instead of having handicapped parents because they have children who are handicapped, we are reversing the "handicapped parent" syndrome.

Profoundly and severely retarded? These words have little or no meaning in such a context.

THE THREE'S AND FOUR'S

Children of three, four, and over have been achieving for a number of years in growth and development centers (day care centers) in many parts of the country in programs sponsored by parent groups and other agencies. Although some of the children are now included in public school programs, many remain in private facilities.

During in-service workshops based on social communication through movement, audiences in various parts of the country are told of the accomplishments of such centers. Hundreds of substantiating statements have been collected. Responses are elicited by the question: "Tell me about a success with the lowest-functioning child you know." A few of these statements are included below; they come from participants who work in growth and development centers in Virginia, Delaware, West Virginia, Maryland, and Pennsylvania, funded by the Department of Health, Education and Welfare (Region III).

I think of children we taught to walk through personal body contact.

Some of my children do not have eye contact. For instance, one little boy appeared to be in a coma for a long time. Suddenly I began to get eye contact. Then a little cerebral-palsied girl needed to learn to eat before I could get any other movement. Then she began to put on weight and began to move her left hand as she heard loud, pounding music.

I think of a "super-favorite" young adult. This was a young lady who was unaware of the world around her and not too aware of herself. I began working with her in the area of dance and through this we eventually got verbalization. Today, I am happy to say, the young lady is fitted with a hearing aid and is able to communicate at a sheltered workshop.

I will tell you about Philip who came to my classroom at the age of seven. Prior to that he merely sat at home. He weighed 95 pounds, was not toilet trained, and had limited speech. Today, Philip has speech, is toilet trained, is able to feed himself, and has lost 15 pounds.

My favorite is a small five-year-old blind-deaf child who, as a result of maternal rubella, was not able to walk or climb. Her parents did not expect success. When I first made a home visit the mother was feeding the child on the floor because she had not been taught to sit in a chair. Today, this child walks to the bus unaided. We found she liked soul music. We got a little portable radio that we held to her ear to encourage her to respond. A disc jockey at a radio station in Annapolis cooperated by playing soul music at certain times of the day.

At three months David was diagnosed as dehydrated and the parents were told he was "on his way out of this world." However, there appeared no reason for him to regurgitate 15 minutes after each feeding. So I thought I was not going to let him get the best of me. I found that he would not regurgitate when left by himself. He was seeking the attention of being given a warm bath and having his clothes changed. We allowed him to be uncomfortable and used cold water to clean him. This he did not like. During the first three days of the new procedure, regurgitation lessened. On the fourth day there was none. Within two months David gained 27 pounds.

I would say that our greatest success is a three-year-old blind retarded child. When she came to us she appeared to be lifeless. The first thing we brought to her was an awareness of the world. Her reaction was crying. It was difficult to convince the parent that crying meant progress for this child. We lived through a period in which nothing we did appeared to reinforce Jill's behaviors. Her hands would draw back. She cried whenever we worked with her. And then we began to find answers. We found that moving her arms and legs helped to quiet her. She listened when paper was crumpled in front of her. Last week we placed a small piano in front of her. As I struck the piano she listened. She reached toward the piano and struck it.

I think of a mother who had transportation problems. Two weeks ago she was quite flushed as she walked into my room carrying Sue. She heard we could help her so she walked three miles to let us begin.

THE SCHOOL-AGED CHILD

Many children from the ages of five to 21 are entering school programs for the first time; some young adults are coming back to continue an interrupted education at 18, 19, or 20 years of age. Perhaps the most significant element to be considered in the entry or reentry of these individuals is the elimination of fear and apprehension on the parts of teachers, parents, and pupils. What parents and teachers need most is an inner security that will also give the pupil confidence in himself. Teachers and parents need to build realistic goals for the child from day to day.

These goals are built quite simply. For instance, one mother told the social worker that her son did not stay dry. "We change him five times a day. What are we going to do?" The social worker's answer is, "Don't worry about it. John will learn. The teacher is prepared. She will observe the times John is dry and help him accordingly."

One mother told about five-year-old Billy's eating habits. Billy "had to be fed." The mother was told to place food in front of Billy, tell him to feed himself, and walk away. The mother and grandmother placed food in front of Billy and said "Eat, Billy." With tears streaming down their faces they walked away. Nothing happened. They continued the same procedure for three days with three meals placed in front of Billy each day. No success. Their pediatrician assured them that Billy would not starve. On the fourth day Billy picked up his food with a spoon and threw it against the wall. On the fifth day Billy began to feed himself. He has been feeding himself ever since.

Sally, an 18-year-old girl, did not chew, or so the teacher was told. She brought baby food each day, until one day the supervisor brought in some finger food. When the baby food was removed, Sally picked up the finger food and fed herself.

One mother told her son's teacher that he would only eat dry food such as potato chips and bread. When the supervisor removed the dry food it took the boy just two days to begin to eat soup and milk and pudding. As might be expected, the liquid food was thrown on the floor the first day; the teacher removed it without comment.

It is not unusual to enter a classroom where the teacher and aide are changing the training pants of children after they arrive on the bus. In a few weeks after the beginning of school many children are toilet trained. Teachers and parents learn to eliminate their own discomfort and anxiety, feelings reflected in the child's actions. They simply replace diapers with training pants, find the reward that can be used to reinforce positive behavior, provide a toilet seat to fit the child, and keep a 24-hour-a-day schedule on toileting in the home and at school.

Obviously there are many ways to reach a child. There is a great deal of useful material on the market, but the teacher must be careful not to impose one particular method without regard for the child's development. The method should not become the end in itself. One teacher began to think of behavior modification as the only way to shape behavior. She rolled a ball to Jeff and he caught it. Jeff got a piece of fudge, his favorite food. The teacher rolled the ball and Jeff caught it . . . a piece of fudge. She rolled the ball again . . . and Jeff regurgitated. Obviously, the fudge was overused as reinforcement.

Since many young adults who left school when they were 16 are returning to stay in school until age 21, teachers and administrators are finding a need to develop special programs. Sheltered workshops are assuming various forms as part of work-study programs in the public schools. Other unique designs are emerging, such as the innovative program of construction projects, initiated by Alvin Sheetz in southwestern Pennsylvania, for which he received an award from the President's Committee on Mental Retardation. In a facility in Sheetz's Intermediate Unit, young women of 18, 19, and 20 spend their school day in a house where they learn to participate in all of the skills of daily living needed in that community. If ready, they move to adult group living homes when they are 21.

There are as many patterns of involvement in this new trend as there are teachers reaching children. Each teacher has his own strengths from which he can build. One is proficient in teaching perceptual and motor skills; another has outstanding ability in physical education. Special skills developed in physical education, art, and music in one state school can be shared with many public schools, and vice versa. Through interschool visits, people learn from each other and in turn develop their own inner securities. In-service education is tailored to the special needs in each county as each develops its own ever-changing curriculum guidelines.

TRANSITION

The value of parents and teachers developing programs for each child out of their mutual understanding has been recognized over the years. Now it is necessary to work together to bring about a transition, which will in turn lead toward programming beginning at birth and continuing throughout an individual's life. Within this transitional phase, structural patterns for immediate needs include: (1) home instruction for the child not able to be transported; (2) integration of one or two severely handicapped children in a class of higher-functioning children; (3) establishment of centers for special instruction of the severely handicapped; and (4) provision of teaching to children in residential settings.

(1) Home instruction. Before the child enters a program in a school building or center, there is an initial home visit by the teacher. Supervisors and teachers then schedule time to work with the child and his parent in the home. In the home visit the teacher learns from the parents; he learns to understand the environment that the child knows. As feelings of trust and security are fostered among the teacher, parent, and child, the concept of the so-called "hyperactive" child is essentially eliminated. When the child is ready for the transition into a school setting, all staff members are prepared to work with him in the new setting.

Some children continue to receive home instruction from the teacher and parent because physical or health factors prevent their traveling. Every effort is made to bring as much of the usual educational stimulation as possible to these children.

(2) One or two severely handicapped children in a "trainable" class. In sparsely settled areas it may be impossible to find enough children to form a workable group of multiply handicapped children within limited chronological ages. One or two severely disabled children may be added to an existing class for higher-functioning trainable mentally retarded. The severely disabled child may be nonambulatory, with abilities as limited as eye contact. Teachers who reach children through the movement of social communication need to be flexible in their approach in such situations that are new to the school situation. The academically oriented teacher has great problems. Too often such a teacher feels the children must sit and stay in their seats, be able to hold a pencil, be able to talk, and perform other activities such as pledging allegiance to the flag. Only through continuing assistance from a knowledgeable supervisor and receptivity on the part of the teacher can there be progress.

(3) Centers for severely or multiply handicapped children. In cities it is possible to have many classes in schools or special centers to accommodate large numbers of children with special needs. In some situations, bus drivers are prepared, through in-service training, to understand the special needs of these children. Trained drivers can teach children to use seat belts and can use special equipment for the nonambulatory child.

(4) Residential settings. Many structural patterns are available for reaching children within different kinds of residential settings. Many children are transported to schools in the community and returned to the residence each day. For children new to a classroom situation, adjustments will be needed to eliminate bizarre behavior that may result from living in large, impersonal institutions. For those unable to be transported for physical reasons, teachers go to the residential setting in which their pupils live. Many students in programs in institutional settings are being prepared for public school placement in the community.

4

Utilizing Human Resources

A teacher planning a curriculum should view the child as an organic entity with every part dependent on other parts. A little growth in stature, in knowledge, in intellect, or in sensitivity affects the child's total pattern of growth. Likewise,

> ... a deficiency in the physical structure, the intellectual ability, and/or the emotional area, has a concomitant limiting effect in terms of the personal effectiveness of an individual in a social setting. (25:1022)*

All facets of development influence patterns of social behavior. The knowledgeable teacher is aware of his own and his students' limitations and the extent to which he must rely on others for information and help. From the physician he learns how a condition or physical difficulty limits an individual. From the psychologist he learns about a child's mental capacity and adjustment status. From the social worker, he finds out about a child's socioeconomic and cultural background. Once the original diagnosis is made, the teacher works with the parents to secure educationally relevant information and to insure a coordinated program between home and school.

*Numbers in parentheses refer to numbered items in the list of selected references. Specific page numbers follow the reference number, after a colon, whenever a reference is quoted directly.

PHYSICAL DEVELOPMENT

The medical diagnosis provides an analysis of the child's physical maturation. It points out such factors as the degree of ambulation, neurological impairment, convulsive disorder, and sensory deficiency. Information from the medical report should be available to help the teacher understand existing physical handicaps, since they affect the child's ability to move and respond to the various physical aspects of an educational program. Does the child have convulsive disorders? If so, the teacher may need to know about the pupil's medication, and have instructions for handling possible seizures. Is the child cerebral palsied? Then the teacher must know how well he is able to move his hands, and under what conditions, to what extent he can walk and climb stairs, and how he can play on the playground. Does he have a neurological impairment that may be responsible for hyperactivity, perseveration, or perceptual difficulties? If so, a neurologist or pediatrician can supply information that will help the teacher meet the child's needs. Is he diabetic? Does he have special dietary problems? Are allergies or asthma present? Is his hearing impaired enough to require a hearing aid, intensive auditory training, special emphasis on language development? Does he need to wear his glasses even when in active physical play? These are some of the areas in which a teacher must have information about the physical condition of each child.

MENTAL AND EMOTIONAL CAPACITY

The psychologist provides an evaluation of mental development, analyzes emotional responses, and aids in the classification of social function as he uses information from psychological examinations in conjunction with data supplied by physician, parent, and social worker. All concerned should exercise extreme caution in using the intelligence quotients (IQ's) of these children. Stull indicates that the relatively inexperienced clinician may be impressed with the seemingly objective nature of the intellectual scale, whereas the experienced clinician, aware of the hazards of classifying on the basis of IQ, particularly with young and/or retarded children, will recognize the importance of the clinician's own sensitivity and astuteness in the effective use of the scale (25:1022).

The child's mental age may have initial value in indicating the level at which he functions intellectually. Used alone, the mental age (MA) gives no indication of what specific items on an intelligence test were answered successfully. It does not differentiate between special needs and lack of experience. However, the skillful psychologist will try to provide information to help the teacher analyze the child's abilities. Some psychologists help the teacher by recommending special techniques to be used in modifying certain behavior.

HOME ENVIRONMENT

The social worker and the psychologist point out elements in the home environment that may have bearing on the success or failure of an educational program: socio-economic status of the family; education of parents; occupations of parents; ethnic or national background; kind of life the family leads; conflicts between parents and siblings. They may explore factors having a direct bearing on the retarded child: the family's attitude toward him; data from hospitals, clinics, and other community agencies; the child's previous schooling, if any; the family's expectations; future planning for the child.

Family and cultural groups exert strong influence over what the child learns. The expectations of adults, the ways in which they attempt to control behavior, the guidance and encouragement they give, and the models they set for imitation influence what the child is allowed to understand. Parents may have a tendency to infantilize or over-protect, to be over-indulgent, or to put undue pressure on the child to achieve skills for which there is little, if any, readiness. Parents may insist that the child learn words by rote—words that are much too advanced for his mental capacity and that have no meaning for him. There may be pressures for "speech correction" before the child has sufficient language to correct. The child's entrance into a school program makes the regular exchange of information between parents and teachers imperative.

CHILD-PARENT-TEACHER RELATIONSHIPS

The conventional concept of parent-teacher relationships, with its connotation of nothing more than occasional meetings, becomes outmoded when parents and teachers join forces to help the child. Group meetings are not sufficient to develop a complete understanding between them, so that they can motivate the child to continue to grow intellectually and emotionally. The child, his parents, and his teacher become inseparably united in their educational efforts. The relationship might be compared to a three-legged milking stool that will collapse if one of its legs is taken away.

In this type of reciprocal arrangement, one parent, or preferably both parents, will visit the classroom for an initial conference with the teacher. The parents describe the child's personality traits, problems, and accomplishments. The teacher tries to obtain information that will be helpful in planning his pupil's school program: his likes and dislikes, how he has been disciplined, the activities and attitudes of the rest of his family. The teacher explains the philosophy and behavioral objectives of the school program. The parents, by observing other children in the classroom, can often begin to understand the meaning of an educational program for their child. Before the child enters school, the teacher visits in the home, not as a "snooper" but to see how differently the child behaves in the two situations, to find out in what activities the youngster has success. The teacher brings Jimmie's "home experiences" to the classroom. Then, when the parents visit the school, they take "school experiences" back into the home.

As the child enters the class, the teacher discusses his program with the child's parents, so that they can coordinate the efforts of home and school. He establishes relaxed communication with the parents by telling them anecdotes of the child's behavior and progress and urging them to do the same to him. "Encourage Pedro to sing the song he learned today in class. . . . Jeanne washed her dishes without being told. . . . Robert does not join in group play. Is he ready for group play? . . . Today was the first day that Marie has not cried at all." In periodic group meetings the teacher and parents discuss common successes and experiences to help the child to the next step in his developmental program.

As teachers and parents work together, they develop skill in observing and reporting to one another. This requires time and artful leadership but pays dividends in helping the child progress toward his best development.

The fruitful effect of such a relationship between parents and teachers is perhaps nowhere more evident than in the case of Mary, a handsome, well-developed seven-year-old, whose appearance was only slightly marred by the residual effect of extensive surgery for a cleft palate. Further operations were planned for the near future to improve the remaining condition. She came by subway to her appointment with the teacher—an embarrassing ordeal for her distraught mother because the little girl's only form of oral expression was a piercing continuous scream. She used this constantly, probably because she found it remarkably effective in making her wishes known. The screaming did not necessarily imply unhappiness or displeasure; she employed it to relate a simple request and even to ask permission. She indulged in tantrum behavior at minor frustrations.

The results of Mary's psychological test indicated that her comprehension was on a much higher level than her speech. She apparently understood many directions but was unwilling to obey them. Although she seemed generally happy and in good spirits, she was constantly negativistic. She resisted every new test item, refusing to try it. Her only major interest during the session was dialing the telephone repeatedly; she seemed fascinated by the rotating wheel and the clicking noise.

Formal testing proved to be impossible because of Mary's demonstrated negativism and resistance. Consequently no valid score could be obtained. From the few items that she did attempt, the psychologist estimated her mental age at 2½ to three years and felt she indicated both a capacity for benefitting from a school experience and a potential for learning. Her speech was at a babbling stage; the cleft palate was considered a major factor in this developmental lag.

On the Vineland Social Maturity Scale, Mary was functioning at the social age of two years, nine months, with a social quotient of 38. Her immature language development and her inability to put on her coat were the factors in which she scored below the three-year level. Mary was still unable to wash her face and hands adequately and to plan cooperatively with other children. She was reported to be quite inventive with toys and rode a tricycle competently.

Mary's case created considerable discussion when her status was evaluated by members of the screening committee prior to recommending her admission to the school situation. They felt that she badly needed the stimulation and discipline of the school environment. At the same time they realized that coping with her screaming and tantrums might prove too difficult in a classroom. Several teachers were asked to review the report on Mary and suggest beginning programs for her.

Of the teachers who studied Mary's report, several stressed the need for observing her in the classroom and possibly at home before formulating a definite program. Several suggested that she be allowed freedom to move about the room at first, to explore and become accustomed to her surroundings. One felt that she should be taken around the classroom and introduced to each child individually, with handshaking encouraged. Most of the teachers agreed that she should be urged to join in the group play, both indoors and out. In the opinion of one teacher, working from the clue regarding her inventive play, Mary might derive satisfaction from the doll corner if steered in that direction. The same teacher felt that singing and fingerpainting might prove to be fruitful pursuits, because of the child's well-developed physical coordination. Several teachers mentioned assigning Mary a simple chore—putting away toys, helping to set the table—so that she might develop a sense of belonging and doing for others. One placed emphasis on grooming and self-care.

The screaming naturally proved a stumbling block for the teachers, but most of them thought it should be ignored as far as possible. One teacher wrote: "I would attempt to subdue her screams and show that this is not the proper means of communication. I would help modify her behavior by establishing limits. I would reinforce the smallest bits of appropriate behavior." A number mentioned the importance of controls, but added that the teacher must not expect too much of the child at first. One suggested placing her next to a well-adjusted child and following established routines.

The actual training that was given to Mary followed the general plans outlined in the replies of the teachers. Her screaming abated appreciably. Her teacher said, in discussing Mary's problem in a teachers' meeting, "I couldn't take the noise away from Mary, but she herself stopped it when she could beat on the drum and participate in large muscle activities at designated times with the more mature pupils of the class. We have to accept children where they are and turn their present patterns into constructive behavior. Before you can delete the unacceptable action, you should have something with which to replace it."

At first Mary's mother brought her to school on the subway and called for her in the afternoon. It would have been unrealistic to expect the driver of the special school bus to care for a child with Mary's unusual behavior problems. Although this proved to be a time-consuming occupation for the mother, the arrangement allowed two interviews a day when mother and teacher could review Mary's progress. After several weeks at school Mary's security increased and the screams subsided gradually.

At that time, the principal suggested that Mary try to go home in the afternoon on the school bus. Both mother and teacher prepared her for the transition. The teacher explained the behavior problem to the driver and advised him to ignore her tantrums whenever possible. According to the teacher's plan, Mary sat next to Jim, with whom she enjoyed building and knocking down block houses. She screamed only once during the initial bus ride; this was caused by excitement at seeing rabbits in a pet shop window. When the other children admired them also, the screams stopped. The experiment proved so successful that after two weeks the teacher considered Mary ready for the morning bus ride. The mother prepared her for the trip, providing, at the teacher's suggestion, a period of quiet before the bus arrived. Once the mother was relieved of the daily trips, she and the teacher communicated with one another through notes in Mary's lunch box. They had weekly conferences for the next few weeks and then shifted to a monthly schedule, with additional meetings if some special need arose. Since Mary's cleft palate hindered vocal production, she underwent further surgery. Later both Mary and her teacher received special guidance from a speech therapist, since there was organic involvement in addition to delayed speech.

Mary, who might easily have become a resident in a custodial setting, was well along the road to adjustment. Her teacher and parents devised a program for her development by drawing on the knowledge, skill, and cooperation of others. But the fulcrum of the program was always the individual child.

5

Assessment and Intervention

Each child has a unique design for growth. To help him, his teachers and parents must first learn to observe and report on his behavior, in order to determine his current level in the various developmental areas. From this assessment will arise the formulation of interventions: that is, it can then be determined what steps should be taken to induce the child's progress to the next stage. In short, teachers and parents need to know what to look for and what to do about it. A comprehensive continuum of teaching and learning during the entire day can thus be provided in play, physical education, art, music, language arts, number concepts, social studies, and science, while the child makes progress in caring for himself, and reaches toward independence in the many home-living and world-of-work skills that he is able to master.

SOCIAL COMMUNICATION THROUGH MOVEMENT

In observing and reporting behavior patterns, teachers and parents must look at the child's social communication as it is evinced through movement. This form of communication permeates the child's evolving self-concept, motor, perceptual and self-care abilities, social interaction, and development of concepts.

Children learn through movement and receptive language long before they express their ideas to others. Through movement the infant and toddler find out about themselves

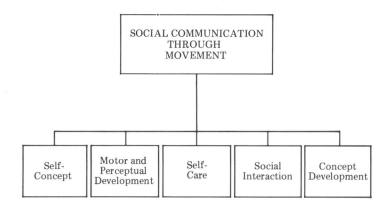

and the world around them. The teenager and the adult continue to reach out and learn more about the world by relating new experiences to past experiences. Teachers, too, will reach a new level of understanding by participating in physical education, music, and art activities that are geared to very low levels of functioning, and to the kinds of movement to which the multiply handicapped child can respond. What a difference there will be in the adult who has learned through role-playing exactly what a certain child with limited movement can and cannot achieve! And what a change takes place in the teacher who finds he can transfer this learning of basic movement patterns to a specific child and see that child move and communicate! Andrews et al. (1:7) express the relationship of the use of movement to thinking processes and other areas of growth as follows:

Movement can be an important factor in learning.

Movement experiences can stimulate thinking.

Movement experiences can help children understand their own ideas and feelings.

Movement experiences can help children develop understanding of other people.

Movement can be a form of communication.

Movement can provide for self-expression.

Movement education can help children develop social interaction.

Movement education can help children develop physical skills in common with unique activities.

Movement education can provide opportunities for cooperation and competition.

Movement education can help children clarify concepts about their environment.

The importance of movement activities based on developmental sequence cannot be overemphasized. Social communication through movement is an integrating force. It is intertwined in all areas. Separating one aspect from another is difficult, yet essential in helping the teacher learn to observe and pinpoint sequences. In actual teaching situations, the parent or teacher can become aware of gains and plan in accordance with his observations in the following areas.

CONCEPT OF SELF

For comprehensive program planning, a systematic evaluation of the mental health of each individual must be made. Each child will be assisted in developing trust and autonomy and in finding people with whom to identify. Teachers and parents require knowledge about how much challenge the child can take before he reaches his frustration level; how the child currently views life; how he handles life situations during moments of crisis; and how he relates to adults, to his peers, and to groups. The child is viewed in terms of his relationship to other people—his adjustment to other children and his position and status with others, his role as an isolationist, leader, or follower in work and play.

The answers to questions like these will help the teacher or parent towards an assessment in this area:

Is there excessive tension, fearfulness?

Does the child relax?

What are his reactions to frustrations?

What drives does he have?

Is there repetitive action, such as rocking?

Does he laugh or smile?

Does he appear to be anxious, compulsive?

Does he trust people?

Does he scream?

Is he withdrawn?

Does he know the parts of his body?

What feelings of satisfaction or dissatisfaction does he have concerning his body?

Does he show indications of success through bodily movement? How?

Do his movements reflect failure, incompetence?

Teachers and parents also need to know how to adjust to the child. Support is required to eliminate unfounded fears in the teacher, the administrator, and the parents, as well as the child. Concerted efforts should be made to eliminate stigma and undue disability labels and to keep labels from becoming permanent.

MOTOR AND PERCEPTUAL DEVELOPMENT

The physical and motor development of the child influences his level of behavior. If there is a developmental lag in this area there are often comparable lags in other functional areas such as perception and cognitive processes. Thus teachers and parents need to be aware of the child's motor abilities so that they can sequence movement activities based upon both his current needs and an analysis of his weaknesses. This awareness can be gained by using any of a number of scales that have been developed over the years by experts in the designation of the various steps in the growth and development of children. Scales of this type include those of Pitcher and Ames (21), Baumgartner and Schultz (5), Haeussermann (11), Stephens (24), and many others. Levels of functioning for young mentally retarded children are suggested by Connor and Talbot (9). Many special educators now use a system of "behavioral objectives" in which the various functional levels are used in developing programs for children. However, behavioral objectives have little value unless the teacher learns to break them down in terms of the minute stages an individual child passes through in learning a procedure. A child may move only a half step, or even a quarter step, at a time. Physical education specialists such as Andrews (1) and others (20) have developed many scales applicable to the specific population with which they work, both in and out of large residential institutions. Teachers can obtain extensive information about these scales, as well as names of numerous curriculum guides containing additional information, from the Educational Resource Information Center (ERIC)*.

SELF-CARE

Children move toward independence and a feeling of security as they learn to do for themselves tasks that adults have been doing for them. The careful observer will see that every child can achieve some measure of success. Toileting and feeding appear to the uninitiated to be of primary concern, as lower-functioning children are added to existing programs. But, as teachers and teacher aides realize that all children can learn, it is amazing to see how much can be quickly accomplished when they work with parents to help the child learn to care for himself both in and out of school. Children need toileting at different times of day and different children need different kinds of assistance. In programs where no accommodation or adjustment is made, children may fail because of rigid scheduling. Progress is made in teaching children to feed themselves as soon as teachers discard their own fearfulness. Examples of such gains are given throughout this book. Another area of concern is that of sufficient rest. For the most part, these children need no more rest than others of the same age. Rest occurs when the child is given a change of pace from quiet to active experiences and vice versa.

SOCIAL INTERACTION

A child who is a newcomer to a class is apt to be socially immature and inactive. He may play in isolation until ready

*CEC Educational Resources Information Center, Reston, Virginia 22070.

to be part of the group. The teacher learns to pick up cues to the child's readiness to be near others rather than forcing him into a group or a circle. The teacher gradually introduces him to situations where he plays near another child or even watches at a distance. Then he may begin to play with a second child; and finally, when ready, with a larger group.

If a child has been pressured at home or if he is not accepted by neighborhood children, he may come to the class filled with frustrations resulting in acting-out behavior. Using the large muscles in strenuous physical exercise may be one means of releasing his frustrations. More acceptable social behavior will emerge as the youngster receives praise, is given responsibility, and generally beings to feel like a useful social being.

Learning about the child's social interaction includes answering such questions as:

How does he play? In an isolated way? In parallel play (near another child)? In associative play with another child? In group activity?

Does he play with other children in his neighborhood?

What readiness does he have for social activities in the classroom?

Is he dependent or independent? If dependent, how can his independence be increased?

The teacher learns about the home of each child in order to choose experiences that will be meaningful to each. For instance, social customs and foods selected by the teacher should conform to the socioeconomic pattern of the community as far as possible. One teacher planned a beautiful fruit cocktail as a special party treat for his inner-city class. To his distress, none of the children touched the unfamiliar delicacy. Learning about home is also helpful in another kind of case. Sometimes overindulgent parents, particularly from upper-income brackets, cater to the child and do not allow him to develop independence. In a home where the child is not permitted to share ordinary household chores (either because servants perform them or because the mother does not want to "burden" the child or take the time to help him), he does not develop a feeling of helpfulness. The teacher works with the parents in exploring useful ways the child can assume responsibility.

The teacher allows the child time and opportunities to explore the world around him. Too often volunteers and aides infantilize the child by doing for him those things he should do for himself. With too many "bodies" hovering over them it is utterly impossible for children to become independent.

THE TEACHER'S CONCEPT OF SELF

In teaching a retarded child, the teacher will often discover as much about himself as he does about the youngster. An immature teacher may blame the student for unsocial behavior, whereas a more mature adult is more likely to look to himself. After ruthless self-examination, the teacher may realize that the reason a certain child throws up is that the teacher communicates no affection to him, or the teacher may discover that he has been too lenient with a child he dislikes, thus keeping the youngster from achieving his quota of independence.

Teachers must accept the possibility of a child's candidly remarking, "Me no like you," and objectively search for the reason behind the statement. They must be secure enough to accept advice from the child's parents. They must know whether they are "getting through" to the child and whether they have explained the program to the parents in an understandable way. If they harbor dislike or resentment for a child, they should take pains to camouflage it skillfully. They must have the ability to correct without anger and to be calm during accidents or misbehavior. They must try to understand what it means to be at the child's level, physically and mentally. When they can no longer motivate a particular child they must face the fact realistically so that the youngster may be transferred.

As the teacher guides the child toward social maturity, he himself will make progress toward this same goal. Progress within themselves was recorded by a number of teachers at the end of their first three weeks of teaching multiply handicapped children. One teacher recorded her thoughts as follows:

> Former attitude: When I first came to my job, I was lost. My previous preparation did not prepare me for these children. We had little equipment and little knowledge of what we were expected to do. When I looked at the children I was shocked and even a little frightened. But I had enough courage to stay with it and approach my job from a day-to-day basis. Somewhere inside of me I knew I wanted to help these children.
>
> Present attitude: I am glad that I gave myself a chance and stayed. I have accepted the children completely. Instead of looking at a group of helpless children, I am looking at beautiful children with personalities all their own. I know some of their likes and dislikes and what I am expected to do with them.
>
> Example of experience: When I first met Jack, I said, "Hi, Jack. How are you today?" Jack became angry. He kicked and cried. It was back to the planning board for Jack and me. Jack appeared difficult to understand. He kept his hands tucked inside his shirt. He spoke to no one but himself. Today I took Jack for a walk. I told him I would take him for a walk if he kept his hands outside his shirt. Jack placed his hands on the arms of his wheelchair. There was a car in the driveway toward which Jack scooted his wheelchair. He spoke to me saying, "Open it"—his first words to an adult. I explained that it wasn't my car but I would take him to my car. When we got to my car Jack said, "Go in car," and with this he raised himself in his wheelchair. I took Jack for a short ride. Our entire trip was completed with Jack's hands outside his shirt. In two weeks' time I became a trusted friend of Jack's and have been able to reach him in a small way.

Another teacher tells of her own progress in the following manner:

> What do you do to make blind eight-year-old Jimmy aware— aware of your presence, aware of his surroundings? I asked myself, what would I do if I were blind? I have other senses. I would use them—touch, for instance. So why not Jimmy? As I took Jimmy out of his chair his arms reached whatever he could find. He found my face. The first time this happened, I did not remove my glasses. The second time I knew what I had to do. I removed my glasses and allowed him to feel my face. His touch was gentle as he found my eyes, hair and nose. Then he felt my closed mouth. He tried to pry it open. I allowed him to put his

hand into my mouth. The second time he stuck his finger into my mouth I bit him gently—enough to keep his hand away from my mouth. He pulled back his hand quickly. This was the first real reaction I got from Jimmy in the two weeks I worked with him. I took him out of the chair and allowed him to crawl on a large mat. He appeared to sense my presence. When he put his hand in his mouth I touched his hand and he removed it. Next week I will try to put him in a walker. Who knows? He may walk by himself one of these days.

Another teacher reported:

In my actual work I have received no guidance but have tried to work on the level of the children. I can't say I've worked successfully nor unsuccessfully. Some days are good. Some are bad. I have learned to love these children and look forward to coming to school each day. I'll tell about some of my rewarding experiences. But keep in mind the fact that each day is different. On the first day I tried to get Mark to transfer blocks from one place to another. Mark would not even sit in a chair. I found out that Mark had just begun to walk. That was àll he wanted to do. So I placed him in front of me and he walked to me. We walk up and down the hall for a short time each day. He stops to hug me and gives me a big smile. He stops to smile at himself in the mirror in the hall, wiggles his feet and places his arms in different positions. He's learning.

Many such changes are occurring as teachers face themselves. In exploring their own attitudes, the answers to these questions will be helpful:

Am I comfortable with this child?

Can I set limits and yet allow this child to grow?

Can I relax with this child?

Am I rigid in my approach?

How will I know when he is ready for a given experience?

Do I accept him where he is?

Do I show irritability with him?

Do I talk about him in front of him? (Even though he has no expressive language he knows what people are saying and reacts accordingly.)

What are my feelings toward him? If negative, do they show?

> Can I get down on his level—sit on the floor and get eye contact, build out of the little successes rather than superimpose adult mannerisms?
> Am I communicating with him?

SUMMARY

When assessment and intervention are applied in combination and carried on continuously, they form a process through which the child makes progress. This progress emerges as a reality for child, parent, and teacher alike, as they advance toward meeting new challenges, building from minute to greater and greater successes—successes undreamed of even two years ago. Quantities of materials are available to enable teachers to develop skill within themselves in the use of this continual building process. The forms included in the appendices of this book are intended to help the college instructor, the supervisor, the uninitiated teacher, or the teacher who is working with lower-functioning children for the first time, to build from one success to the next, with no limit in sight. Who can say what the child's potential is, or what the teacher's potential for reaching him will be tomorrow?

6

The School Environment

The school environment, which provides for the child's physical, intellectual, emotional, and social needs, extends beyond the classroom. It provides for interaction in the school building, home, and community. Since human beings perceive environments differently and have unique ways of learning in terms of their own purposes and understandings, the school environment must be structured so that each child has access to the space, time, equipment, materials, people, and activities necessary for his growth and development.

SPACE TO MOVE

The physical growth of children with limited mental ability is generally similar to that of other children. They have a basic need for motor activity that will enable them to gain control of their bodies and develop greater coordination. They need space for movement, for stretching, and for letting go (1). They express their thoughts and feelings through their bodies. Space makes it possible for them to learn through experimentation and to clarify confusions about their environment. When they are given sufficient opportunities to use movement they react to the world about them and use movement as a means of communication in expressing their innermost thoughts and feelings.

Since movement is such a prime factor in a program for mentally retarded youngsters, a spacious room is of the utmost importance. The floor of the room should be covered or at least partially covered with carpeting for the children and teacher to sit on, move, and use their bodies in gross motor activity. Mirrors should be added—full-sized mirrors placed vertical to the floor for the ambulatory child, and long plexiglass mirrors placed horizontal to the floor for the young or nonambulatory child who crawls to the mirror. If tables or desks are used they should be grouped against a wall, not set in rigid lines. Cots should be available when children need a rest but should be stored when not in use. School tables and chairs fit the size and needs of the child and special furniture is provided for the nonambulatory child. A beanbag chair (a large, closed sack of leather or leatherlike material, loosely filled with beans or some similar stuffing, which can be formed or pushed into the shape or height desired) is useful in many classes. Special toilet equipment is fitted to the needs of children who are handicapped physically or who need facilities of different sizes.

TIME

The child's body will determine his movement and his expression. It will determine the amount of time he needs to complete an activity or to move from one place to another. It will affect the length of time he needs to make the transition from one pursuit to another. It will determine the amount of rest he needs and the amount of vigorous play he can take. The child himself is usually the best guide to the length of time he can participate in any one activity. The danger of a child's overtaxing his strength is slight when the teacher gauges his timing from clues he takes from the child. Which youngster is last to finish a particular activity? How soon after a game starts does lame Jeannie become fretful? The teacher will learn how much time to allow and to balance allotments between vigorous and restful activities.

The teacher recognizes the uniqueness in the language development of each child in his group and plans time for each one to communicate in his own way. He allows time to help the child interpret his experiences, enabling him to "get outside" himself and to interact with other members of the group.

MATCHING MATERIALS TO CHILDREN

The teacher plays a supportive and guiding role in helping the children work toward solutions of their own problems as far as they are capable of solving them. The children are encouraged to live out their experiences in simple gross motor activities, in caring for themselves, in dance, music, and art. They use materials creatively in their own ways rather than in imitation of set adult patterns. The members of a class need a variety of materials from which to choose. They need materials which are within their capabilities but at the same time challenge their skill and imagination.

By careful observation the teacher will become aware of individual and group needs. Some of the finest matching of materials to children's needs is found among teachers who get to know the child at home and at school before ordering special materials. Obviously, teachers will often go without commercial materials for a period of time because school districts require that orders be placed months before they are delivered, but ingenious teachers can meet special needs through things found in the home. For instance, a teacher may say, "I have no materials. Look at what I have to use!" The reply might be, "Be glad you do not have to use the stockpiles of commercial materials some other person ordered. They would be stored in your already bulging closet because they were of no immediate value. The coffee can into which Johnny is dropping clothespins is bringing Johnny to life. Look at the change in Jen as she carries the large purse, zips and unzips it, puts in a key ring with keys and crawls in front of the mirror." Other ideas include:

- Developing movement on rugs, foam mats, all-purpose mats.
- Providing tactual stimulation with cellophane, tissue, squeeze toys, wood, metal, dry and wet sponges, blocks and sticks, rubber toys, kitchen spatulas,

brushes, cloth, plastic bottles with screw and snap lids, and with items having different textures for rubbing, scraping, thumping, scratching.

- Developing grasp with objects of different textures, sizes, shapes, and sounds that will motivate the child to want to reach and play.
- Developing locomotor skills by placing masking tape on the floor in different designs for children to follow; placing footprints cut from contact paper on the floor; making an obstacle course that calls for crawling under tables and chairs.
- Developing confidence through bodily contact; rubbing the child's back; sitting in a large rocker and holding the child while rocking; letting the child use a small rocker.
- Providing auditory stimulation with drums, handbells, cowbells, toys with purring motors.
- Developing sensory stimulation with bubbles, pinwheels, whistles, feathers for blowing.
- Developing feeding skills through use of special spoons, easy grip utensils, peanut butter placed on the roof of the child's mouth, finger foods for the child not able to feed himself with utensils, finger painting with puddings.
- Developing coordination through the use of various materials while music is played, such as streamers of various colors tied to a limb the child can use, flags (colored cloth tied to a stick) to wave, heavy dowel rods cut in different sizes to pound on the floor.
- Developing gross motor abilities with balls: big balls, small balls, balls to hold, push, kick, or punch, beach balls, and large balls suspended from the ceiling.
- Having the room suitable for exploring, by removing any item that might break and allowing the children to touch anything they want.

Remember storage space requirements in your plans. Listings such as this need to be modified in terms of the individual children within a group. Each teacher will think of better materials to meet the special needs of his pupils; the room will reflect the personality of the boys and girls in the class. Standard materials for various activities are listed below.

Art

Painting accessories—poster paints, finger paints, small jars for paints, assorted long-handled brushes, easels

Drawing materials—colored chalk, charcoal, crayons (large size for young children)

Paper—newsprint 18" x 24", manila paper, construction paper in assorted colors, large wrapping paper, newspapers; paper bags

Clay equipment—clay (dry or moist by pound or tub), clay pail with cover, clay boards

Sawdust

Miscellaneous art accessories—scissors, paste, shellac, stapler with staples, punch, pipe cleaners, clothes-pins

Sewing materials—needles, thread, buttons, cloth, thimbles

Water drawing equipment—sponges, small buckets

Magazines

Oilcloth

Music

Record player and records

Piano

Song books and sheet music (for teacher)

Block Play

Large hollow blocks

Floor or unit blocks

Playhouse blocks

Table blocks

Accessory materials to use with blocks: toy trucks, cars, houses, garages, figures of people

Doll House Corner

The doll house corner is closely related to children's family life. Here they can play out well-known roles. Materials include:

Kitchen equipment—stove, refrigerator, sink, cabinet, pots and pans
Dining equipment—table with chairs, set of dishes
Household furniture—beds, chairs, chest of drawers
Cleaning supplies—mop, broom, dustpan and brush
Ironing board and iron
Dolls and doll clothes
Dress-up clothes

Woodwork

A workbench and some tools should be an integral part of every classroom for the trainable mentally retarded. The younger children always enjoy hammering and sawing soft wood, and older ones use many tools. The abilities of the individual children and the training of the teacher determine how much they accomplish. Suggested equipment includes:

Workbench with vises (correct height for the children in the class)
Storage cabinet or special board for storing tools
Tools—hammers (correct size for each group), crosscut saw, coping saw, screwdriver, tri-square, plane, clamps, rulers, pliers, hand drill with bits, soft wood, sandpaper (assorted), doweling (assorted), glue, nails (assorted), screws

Picture and Story Books

Attractive picture books and story books with realistic illustrations that children understand are a source of enjoyment in the library corner of the room. Children go to the library and select their own books with the help of the teacher or librarian. Also, the teacher uses the books to prepare and follow up experiences where the children think, feel, see, hear, and express themselves.

Indoor and Outdoor Activities

Materials are selected to meet the needs of various ages to enable children to entertain themselves at school and at home. Parents send some ideas; the community abounds in others. A few suggestions:

Balls of all sizes (depending on size, coordination, and needs of children)—huge push-ball (as large as some children), light rubber balls, volleyballs, basketballs, softballs (for older children)

Table games—Bingo, Lotto, other matching games, puzzles, dominoes, card games such as Old Maid

Puppets

Tinker Toys

Bean bags

Colored cones and cubes

Pick Up Sticks game

Sand and Water

Children enjoy using indoor sand tables and outdoor sandpiles. Water play is fun for little children. They enjoy drawing with a wet sponge on the blackboard or playing with light, waterproof toys in a pail of water. Needless to say, they should be taught to clean up after such play and to store the equipment. Suggested materials include:

Containers—large pans, tubs, pails and shovels

Sprinklers (outdoors)

Miscellaneous equipment—molds, spoons, sponges, large brushes, soap, bubble pipes, hollow blocks, waterproof toys

Outdoor Equipment

Children need places to use their large muscles outdoors even more, if possible, than indoors. They need to climb, run, jump, push, and pull things. Storage space for all outdoor eqiupment should be adjacent to the outdoor play area if possible.

Playground equipment—swings, sliding board, jungle gym, ladders, steps, gaily painted pipes (to crawl though)

Wading pool
Locomotion toys—wagons, scooters, tricycles
Jumping ropes
Rubber tires on ropes
Sawhorses and boards
Hollow blocks
Packing boxes

Household Arts

The younger child learns to stack his dishes. The older child prepares his lunch. Shopping trips and special errands provide clues to his stage of development. Standard equipment, which should fit the size of the children involved, includes:

Kitchen stove, refrigerator, sink with hot and cold running water, cupboards
Eating materials—dishes, silverware, glasses, napkins
Kitchen accessories—cooking utensils, toaster, dish towels
Ironing board and iron
Special spoons, knives, forks for the severely handicapped.

Housecleaning Supplies

The younger children learn to put the room in order after each activity. The older children learn the responsibilities of cleaning an entire house, which provides an excellent way for the child's schooling to carry over into the home. Standard supplies include:

Broom and dustpan
Wet mop and bucket
Wastebasket
Sponges, soap and detergents, cleanser

SUMMARY

The school environment is attractive when it includes the resources necessary for the child's growth and development. An uncluttered appearance with plenty of plain wall space provides a suitable background for developing self-control, composure, and orderliness. The organization and placing of permanent equipment is thoughtfully planned indoors and outdoors. Enough space is provided so that activities do not crowd each other. The child's body and tempo determine his kind of movement and expression. Materials and equipment help him meet a variety of needs and present a challenge to his skill and imagination.

7

The Child Enters the Classroom

When the TMR child enters the structural environment of the classroom he brings with him experiences that relate to his home, his parents, and limited areas outside his home. All these experiences serve as guidelines for the teacher in programming, for the child needs step-by-step assistance in making the transition from home to school. Teachers and parents must forge links between the two environments. Some children are ready to leave their mothers as they board the school bus on the first day of school. Others may need their mothers' support on the first day of school, during the entire first week, or even for the first month.

The teacher cautiously studies the child and helps in this transition kindly but firmly. Even though an individual is severely retarded, his propensity for finding out "how far the teacher will allow him to go" is similar to that of any child. A child who is fond of kicking when she does not get her own way will kick the teacher unless he stops her. Teachers must establish control, distracting students by substituting an acceptable activity and warmly approving more desirable behavior. If necessary, students are physically removed from the situation.

Whatever a child's chronological age, the teacher follows the same formula used for a child of normal intelligence—that is, to stop, distract, and approve. The behavior may be just as typical when an overprotected child of sixteen "tries out" a new teacher as it was when he was six, and the remedy will prove just as applicable.

In some instances, ignoring attention-getting devices is the best way to guide a child away from objectionable conduct. For example, Todd was a child who needed this kind of treatment. Accustomed to using vile language to get attention from his parents, Todd on numerous occasions called his teacher a socially unacceptable name. To his amazement, he did not get the expected response. He then tried screaming and was not reprimanded, but simply ignored. After three weeks Todd began to go out of his way to seek his teacher's praise, storing blocks on shelves after playing with them. He even tapped a girl on the shoulder to remind her that it was time to clean up. The vile language and screaming gradually gave way to more acceptable behavior as Todd relaxed and felt secure within the school situation.

Basic routines through which the newly admitted child can orient himself give stability to life at school. Such routines may include designated times for lunch, outdoor play, music, art, and free play. The child will learn that all children in his group come into the building together. He will learn that all the children wash their hands before eating. Basic structures provide the foundation for security through which the child can find flexibility to meet his own needs. Jim, for instance, needs to learn that all members of his class remain in the classroom for certain periods of the day; they do not open the door and run down the hall. The blocks in the corner are not used for throwing, but may be used to build houses, like the apartment house where Jim lives.

As the child begins to adjust from home life to school life, the teacher's program becomes more flexible and more options are available to both the teacher and the child. The teacher organizes the content of the program, selecting meaningful experiences and interpreting situations in a way that the child can comprehend. Toileting is planned to meet individual needs. Special planning is needed for the child who has not learned related self-help skills.

The teacher serves as a model. If he wants a child to express himself, he copies the child's movements and sings for the child and with him. If he wants the child to talk, he listens; he provides movement and experiences for the child and waits for the child's own reactions. The teacher lives experiences with the child by moving out into the community where they ride on buses and boats, see airplanes, shop, go to the zoo, swim, roller skate, see baby farm animals, see the buds about to burst forth on the trees in the park, build a snowman. In all neighborhoods there are rich experiences for planning and doing.

No two children will react in exactly the same way; each is an individual with individual experiences and a design for growth and development. Each child's parents have ways of living different from others; each teacher has strengths and weaknesses of his own; each community is somehow unique. One of the factors on which the extent of this child's growth and development depends is the consideration given to these individual differences in background. The child's present stage in all developmental areas must be ascertained, and his experiences planned accordingly. In their interactions with him, teachers and parents must have realistic expectations, and should be aware of themselves in terms of what they have to offer him. In the classroom, a teacher with musical talent may have success with songs and other musical activities, an athletic teacher with games and outdoor sports, a dramatically talented teacher with skits, puppetry, role-playing. No program will be uniformly successful in all of its details for any two children.

The schedules below present glimpses of children as teachers help them grow and develop.

A DAY WITH YOUNG CHILDREN

Eleven children with special needs are in their fourth week in a day care center with 40 other children in an inner city area. These children range in age from 18 months to four years, five months. For the past year, the group had been housed in a separate facility a few blocks away for children considered mentally retarded. The teacher, the teacher aide, and the parents of these children worked together helping them at home and at school. After weeks of negotiating, they convinced the Board of Directors of a general day care center that the children with special needs could be integrated with the regular children. Miss May, the teacher, Mrs. Giles, the teacher aide, and the parents became part of the regular day care center as they worked together in tailoring the facilities and the program to the eleven children while integrating these children into the mainstream of the larger day care program. Miss May, Mrs. Giles, and the parents had visited the center, spoken with other teachers, and observed the regular children before the eleven special children came to the center. A room was selected near the entrance to the building. This particular classroom has all the features of the rooms occupied by the other early childhood groups: for example, a lavatory with equipment of a suitable size is adjacent to the room. Like the other classrooms, it has built-in shelves, quantities of large and small blocks, a well-equipped housekeeping corner, a piano and record player, a library corner with colorful picture books, a dress-up center with clothes, a bulletin board, bicycles, tricycles, large balls, and other outdoor equipment on an adjacent playground. There are large spaces for movement indoors and out. A special ramp has been built to accommodate wheelchairs; carpeting covers the floor; mirrors are horizontal to the floor. Teacher-prepared instructional materials are added each day to meet emerging needs.

The transition to the new location was made gradually. The teacher prepared the children by taking them to visit the new center during the week before the move. The boys and girls helped in packing. Parents discussed the move at home, and took their children to and from the center for the first few days. Gradually, the children learned to ride the buses with the other children. Parents continue to bring two-year-old Sidney and three-year-old cerebral-palsied Judy. These children were new to the program six weeks ago. They will be ready to ride the bus in a short time.

Three-year-old Marty and four-year-old Sue have left Miss May and are now in the regular day care program. In fact, they appear more competent than most of the children in their group. Their new teacher is using the detailed information she received from Miss May concerning the step-by-step learning of these children. Five-year-old Jim is spending two hours each day in a new group. He returns to Miss May for special work on motor coordination and movement. He finds it difficult to climb stairs by himself and needs assistance.

Since Mary began to relate to a friend from her neighborhood who rides her bus, she spends time playing in the housekeeping corner with her friend in the regular class. The teachers are observing this new development. Miss May is recording Mary's progress in other skills that will be needed before she can be moved to the regular group on a full-time basis.

Mrs. Giles and the parents use special procedures as needed in toilet training for four of the children. This includes toileting when the child gets up, after breakfast, when he arrives at school, and at frequent intervals as required throughout the day. One of the four is almost completely trained. He is incontinent only at night after undue excitement before retiring.

Jack, who is in a wheelchair, has eating problems. He is learning to eat with a special spoon that is attached to his wrist. Special techniques are used to reinforce his behavior.

In a short time other children with special needs (now on a waiting list) will be brought to Miss May, who will find out from the parents where the child has success and where he needs special help. Miss May and Mrs. Giles will work with each child and prepare special materials to be used at home with advice from the school. Each of these boys and girls will be integrated into the mainstream when they are ready. When needed, Mrs. Giles and Miss May help the other teachers plan and carry out special experiences.

Miss May's flexible schedule includes activities within categories such as those listed below. She is mindful of sequencing procedures to meet special needs and uses every opportunity to build the day-by-day teacher-prepared materials.

Sample Schedule

8:20-8:45 Buses arrive. Toileting as needed.
8:45-9:15 Supervised free play.

9:35-10:00 Transition. Moving to music. Songs, finger plays, special ideas related to each child's reactions during the past half hour.

10:00-10:15 Toileting as needed. Mid-morning snack, cleanup.

10:15-11:00 Gross motor activities. Half of period devoted to special activities to meet individual needs and other half to free choice on large equipment.

11:00-11:30 Art, language arts, and specially prepared materials.

11:30-Noon Transition. Putting room in order. Toileting as needed. Setting table or going to cafeteria.

Noon-1:00 Lunch. Special eating procedures, conversation, cleanup.

1:00-2:00 Naps. Those not needing rest on cots play in a part of the room removed from cots. When individuals awake they go outdoors with teacher aide, or move to the other side of the room where they engage in quiet activities.

2:00-3:00 Toileting as needed. Individualized activities. Free choice for those not engaged in individualized work.

3:00-4:30 Supervised play, outdoors when possible, with special motor activities sequenced to individual needs.

4:30-5:30 Time to clean up, replace equipment, tell "what I did today," "what I will tell mother," and "what I will do tomorrow." Prepare room for next day. Time to use the lavatory, help in dressing, and talk about the bus ride going home.

A DAY IN A PRIMARY CLASS

P.S. 6 is located in a residential section of an average-income neighborhood in a city with a population of 25,000. The primary class is in a self-contained room. The room has toilet facilities, hot and cold running water, a housekeeping corner with cupboard, stove, table, chairs, a dressing table, dishes, and dress-up clothes. Open-shelved storage space contains blocks of varying sizes. Tables and chairs are placed on one side of the room, allowing sufficient space for movement near the piano and record player.

The classroom adjoins a kindergarten room on one side and a first grade on the other. The children enjoy dancing with the neighboring classes. The class in question is one of three in the city for special children of this chronological age. The others are in different school buildings. All the children are transported by school buses. Three children come from outside the city where districts contract for services because there are not enough children in their communities for classes within the four-year age range. With two exceptions, the children come from middle-income homes. The parents visit the school often and are active participants in programming. Some of the mothers and fathers have become astute observers and reporters of child behavior.

This special class consists of ten children. They range in age from five years, two months to eight years, one month. Two children have a history of convulsive seizures. One youngster wears a short leg brace. One child is legally blind, but has limited light perception. Communication consists of single words by four of the children, gestures by two, babbling by one, "Ah, ah," by one, and phrases by two. The class has been in existence for five months. Four of the children joined in the first week of school, two each in the second and third weeks, and one each in the third and fifth months.

Sample Schedule

8:30-9:00 Preparation for the day by the teacher. The reports and anecdotal records that are available to the teacher provide clues to planning for each child. The teacher carefully plans each detail of classroom routine in terms of the comprehension of the youngsters. A "helper chart" is placed in a prominent place, with a paper plate drawn next to Nancy's name, a block next to Mary's, and a milk carton next to Sammy's. Nancy, Mary, and Sammy can recognize their names in manuscript writing and are ready to assume their respective responsibilities for setting the table before juice period and lunch, storing blocks after free play, and pouring milk for lunch. Dress-up clothes are available in one center of interest. Rugs are placed on the floor at one end of the room for "Show and Tell." The juice is poured into a container that Arnold can handle and a box of crackers is ready for another child to serve. Two easels covered with paper, large easel brushes, and paint are readily accessible.

9:00-9:30 Removal of wraps, free play, individual needs. The teacher meets the children as they arrive and climb from the buses—gesturing, waving, their attitudes reflecting what happened at home before the bus arrived. Ira, a Down's syndrome child, points to his new shoes. Mona, the little blind girl, rises from her seat and reaches out for assistance as she leaves the bus. Alice babbles, "Me, me, me," as she pushes her lunch box to the teacher, indicating that a note from mother is in the box. (The note gives information from the doctor about a new medication to keep Alice's seizures under control.) Carolyn is the last child to leave the bus because of the brace on her leg. The children follow the teacher up the stairs to the classroom. Nancy, Mary, and Sammy remove their coats, move quickly to the chart to determine their duties for the day, and then go to the block corner where they begin to build. Freddy, a seven-year-old brain-injured child, is new to the group and needs help getting started. The teacher takes a firm hold on his hand, guiding him toward the classroom. After helping the little boy with his wraps, the teacher leads him to the workbench to a pounding toy. Freddy grasps a hammer and begins to pound. While the teacher gives attention to some of the other less capable children, he continues to keep an eye on Freddy. He sees Freddy leave the workbench and wander about the room exploring. When Freddy reaches out to pinch Nancy, the teacher quickly removes him from the situation and places him on a rug next to the teacher in the corner where the children are assembling to "Show and Tell." Ira twirls in the foreground, pointing to his new shoes as he moves from child to child. The teacher keeps his left hand free to limit Freddy's unsocial behavior; with the other hand he jots down (on small pieces of paper that he carries in his pocket) the clue he recognizes in Arnold's helping Carolyn sit on the rug next to him. This marks the first time that Arnold's observed actions have been related to another child. After each child shares interests with the group, the teacher tells a story about Mary (whose movements indicate she is losing interest). He illustrates the story on a large sheet of newsprint:

Mary came to school today.

She came on a bus.

Mary brought her lunch box with her.

Mary walked up the stairs.

(At the end of the day the teacher folded Mary's picture story into her lunch box to take home with her.) After Mary's story, other children ask to have stories told about them. Mona beams as she handles the objects used in her story:

> "Mona will drink milk today." (A milk carton is placed in Mona's hand.)
> "She will drink with a straw." (Mona reaches for a straw.)

On this particular day, most of the children moved readily into the activities, but sometimes nobody seems inspired to start the day's routine. Occasionally the entire program may be disrupted as it was yesterday, when the teacher was not prepared for Freddy's first day at school and the other children became excited as the new child moved about the room trying to upset their projects. Today, however, the teacher is prepared and knows better how to set limits on his hyperactivity.

9:30-10:00 Snack time. The children prepare for this by using the toilet and then washing their hands. The more capable youngsters care for themselves, but Freddy and Alice receive special assistance. The teacher sings and the verbal children add their sounds: "We wash our hands, we wash our hands. . . ." While the others are getting ready, Nancy and Sammy set the table. Arnold gets the juice from the refrigerator and pours it. Mary puts the crackers on a dish. After all are seated around the table, with Freddy next to the teacher, Arnold pours the juice. Mary passes the crackers, carefully pushing Mona's hand toward her cracker. There is an "Ank u" from Nancy. Freddy throws a cracker on the floor but retrieves it when the teacher says firmly, "Freddy, get down and pick it up—right now." After most of the children have finished the snack (Mona is allowed to finish hers at her own speed), the children listen to the teacher talk about the new push-ball that arrived the previous day—"the ball that is as big as we are." Jim says, "Uh, uh, uh," excitedly as he goes through the motions of pushing, and Mary adds, "Me push."

10:00-10:30 Outdoor play. Since the day is pleasant, the

children put on their coats preparatory to playing outside. Freddy tries to place his arms in one sleeve; he had been unable to do this on the first day of school. Once outdoors, all the children try to push the ball around the playground. Freddy continues to push the ball even after the others begin a circle game. Later some of the children play on the jungle gym, swings, and slide. Arnold wanders over to an older group and tries to join in the ball game. Freddy still pushes the ball about the playground by himself (a clue for the teacher). A few minutes before the end of the period, the teacher leisurely begins to assemble the group preparatory to returning indoors. Arnold and Freddy, the newest additions to the program, have to be brought to the group by Mary and Tommy. On the way into the classroom, Carolyn's excited "Uh, uh, uh" attracts everyone's attention to a steam shovel a short distance from school. The teacher, aware of the time limitation, asks the children if they would like to visit the steam shovel after their rest period.

10:30-10:45 Quiet period. The children have a change of pace on their return to the classroom, where the teacher plays soft music. Some of the children look at picture books of their own selection, while others rest at the table with their heads on their hands.

10:45-11:30 Finger plays, music, art. With the exception of Freddy and Arnold, the children move to the teacher, who sits on the floor and begins to recite a finger play while moving his body: "I push the ball, I push the ball, I push, I push, I push." The children nearby join in the movement. Sammy, who is more articulate than the others, recites the end of the lines with the teacher. Other children ask for other finger plays with gestures. As the teacher touches the piano the veterans in the program come to life, responding with appropriate movement as they recognize the "walking music," the "running music," the "jumping music." The newcomers watch from the sidelines or try to get attention by gurgling noises. The teacher suggests that they make up a Freddy song. They begin by saying, "FRED-dy, FRED-dy," with accent on the first syllable. Two children use rhythm sticks, another a drum, while the teacher plays it on the piano and the other children attempt to sing it. Then the children participate in familiar songs according to their wishes—by beating time, dancing, singing. Following this period of activity, in which the children have used their large muscles, a less strenuous occupation is needed. They return to the tables where the teacher has laid out large sheets of paper for finger painting. Mona gingerly daubs the paint on the paper with one finger while Ira delves into his paint with both hands. Freddy tastes his.

11:30-12:30 Scrub up and lunch. The more capable assume responsibilities by setting the table, getting milk from the refrigerator, and placing chairs around the table. The children gradually get ready for lunch, each moving at his own pace. Most of them can eat without assistance, but the teacher is conscious of those who might need help, placing these youngsters near him if possible. During the leisurely lunch the children communicate with each other in various ways. On some days direction is needed, as on the day Tommy intentionally upset Mary's milk to get attention. During the first few days of the class, routines required more time than now, since the children had to become accustomed to their new surroundings and to eating by themselves.

12:30-1:00 Quiet, free choice period. The transition is casual and gradual. To the accompaniment of quiet music from the record player, Arnold and Ira look at pictures; Mary, Tommy, and Alice build with large blocks; Mona rocks back and forth on the edge of her chair; the teacher ventilates the room. The more capable play a quiet game. Hearing the teacher praise Mary for her work, Ira gets the broom and says, "Ook, me weep."

1:00-2:30 Field trip plans and preparation for departure. Alice leads Mona to the housekeeping corner where she tries to help Mona dress a doll. The other children finish storing free choice material. Carolyn tugs at the teacher's hand, pointing toward the steam shovel and says, "Uh, uh, uh!" The teacher responds by a smile and then talks about how they will cross the street for their second planned excursion outside the school yard. (Earlier in the year they walked around the block to see Nancy's home.) As they put on their wraps the teacher gives each child instructions for safety—holding hands, looking in both directions for cars, crossing the street together. Nancy and Mary join hands as leaders and the others follow suit. The teacher, grasping Freddy's hand, walks beside the group. The little expedition is a great success. The operator, pleased at a break in his routine, explains to the group how the big machine works and lifts Ira into the driver's seat. (For days after the visit the children dramatized the steam shovel action and Ira strutted about in his new role of steam-shovel man.) When they return to the classroom there is time for free play, followed by toileting and a quiet period with soft music. When preparations for going home begin, Carolyn gives the teacher a pencil and goes through the motions of writing; she wants a note telling her mother about the steam shovel.

2:30-3:00 Recording observations. The teacher studies his scribbled notes of the day's accomplishments—Freddy's interest in the push ball, Carolyn's "Uh, uh, uh" in response to the steam shovel, Arnold's taking Carolyn's hand. He records these clues so that he will not forget them as he plans activities for the next few days. He considers possibilities for creative steam shovel rhythms. He plans to give Freddy the responsibility for storing the ball, after the child has become accustomed to the classroom situation. Before leaving for the day, the teacher jots down memoranda of things he wants to discuss with parents of various children in the class.

A DAY IN AN INTERMEDIATE CLASS

Miss Jones teaches one of three classes for children with retarded mental development in a 900-pupil elementary school in a large city. Her class has a regular-sized room on the second floor between two other similar classes, one for younger children and one for older ones. They are fortunate in having a room near a gym.

Of the ten children in the class, six have been in the program for a year and a half, three entered at the beginning of the present year, and one joined the class three weeks ago. The newcomer, who is on a six-week trial period, is the son of a foreign diplomatic official; his schooling is complicated by the fact that he hears no English spoken at home.

Chronological ages range from nine years, three months to 12 years, one month. One-third of the group have Down's syndrome. Medical and psychological reports indicate a history of brain injury for two of the group. One child, Jim, has a fear of stairs. At this time the teacher and administrator feel that Jim has a chance of profiting from the program because recently he began to move about the room without holding on to chairs and tables. Miss Jones even got him to throw a ball to her. Most of the children come from homes of a low socioeconomic level; the teacher is beginning to establish rapport and understanding with the parents. Most of the children in this class are beginning to express themselves and to understand what they can do.

Sample Schedule

8:30-9:00 Miss Jones checks to see that all gym equipment is in readiness for the first activity. She displays the children's drawings of the United Nations building on the bulletin board. (The class had taken a bus to visit the United Nations the previous week because "Juan's father works there.") She places recordings on the table by the record player and fresh sheets of paper on the easels with water color containers and brushes. She checks hangers to see that each child's apron is ready for work with clay.

9:00-9:45 Arrival; gym. Miss Jones meets the buses as they arrive from various parts of the city. Most of the children get off the buses and climb the stairs with the other retarded children. Because Jim is afraid of the stairs, Miss Jones stays behind with him, takes his hand, and talks in a relaxed manner about the "fine way" he threw the ball yesterday. Cautiously and laboriously Jim begins to mount the stairs with a questioning look in his eyes. The children remove their wraps, hang them up, and check the charts to find their responsibilities for the day. Miss Jones explains that the weather is too cold for outdoor play, so they will play in the gym today. All the children except Jim and Juan move to the storage space for sneakers and begin to change shoes. Some need help in having shoestrings tied. (This intricate manual skill is usually the last bit of self-care learned by any child.) For the first time Harold removes his shoes all by himself because he does not want to miss any of the fun. Yesterday Miss Jones asked Harold to sit on the bench in the gym for part of the period because he made no attempt to help in removing his shoes. Miss Jones gets Juan's sneakers and asks him, in motions, to change his shoes; she has to use sign language since Juan is unfamiliar with English. Then she finds Jim's sneakers and helps him change into them. Two of the girls get the jumping ropes and two of the boys carry the volley balls as they go to the gym. Then they unroll the tumbling mats on the floor. Miss Jones carefully watches for clues in the gross muscle activities of the various children. They run, tumble on the mats, throw balls, each child releasing pent-up energy from the long bus ride and earlier frustrations. After this initial bit of free play, Miss Jones begins a circle game with the girls and boys. All but Jim join the circle. Noticing this, Miss Jones leaves the circle and encourages Jim to throw the ball "like a big boy, the way you did yesterday."

9:45-10:45 Group and individual communication. The children change their shoes on their return to the classroom and gradually take their places in a circle with Miss Jones. Before joining the circle Juan points to the picture of the United Nations building, and Miss Jones explains again, "Yes, that is where Juan's father works." Each child coming into the group expresses in some way the activity of the gym. Elaine says, "Me ball." Jim anxiously waits to hear some praise for his efforts. After a chance to react to early morning experiences, the children carry the chairs to tables where they match objects to pictures, learn to print their names in manuscript letters, or engage in other "school"-type activities for which some are ready. One child uses a sand tray in writing with his finger, while another tries his name at the blackboard. All except two begin a homemade Bingo game of matching well-known pictures relating to excursions they have made into the community. Mary calls the names of the pictures and the others respond with single words or phrases, "I," or "I have it," as they cover the pictures on their cards. Juan wanders to the bulletin board.

10:45-11:00 Free play and toileting. Children play by themselves or in small groups on their return to the classroom from the lavatories.

11:00-11:30 Music and rhythms. As the teacher plays soft music on the record player the children store toys, blocks, equipment, and move the chairs to side of room in preparation for the music period. They sit on the floor and sing familiar songs. Then, as the teacher plays the piano, they move about the room to "structured music"—walking, running, skipping, hopping. They become creative as Miss Jones plays the piano and asks, "Who wants to be a bear?" "How does the fireman walk?"

11:30-12:00 Art. Two of the children help Miss Jones distribute the clay boards and large quantities of clay. Some of them just roll the clay. With encouragement they begin to express their ideas concerning the bus in which they rode on the special trip, and other such interests.

12:00-12:20 Clean-up, preparation for lunch. With few exceptions each child cares for his needs as he prepares for lunch.

12:20-12:50 Lunch. The children go to the cafeteria where they get their trays and food just as the other children do. They all eat at their own table under Miss Jones' supervision. (Learning to follow cafeteria procedure required a great deal of practice, time, and patience at the beginning of the program.)

12:50-1:20 Quiet free choice period. The children visit Mrs. Gray's classroom, where they choose special group games or activities, thus enabling Miss Jones to have her rest period. One child turns on the record player while two girls dance. Others work on puzzles or choose books on special interests prepared by the teacher. One child stays behind to prepare a bulletin board.

1:20-1:50 Special needs. The period immediately after returning to their own classroom Miss Jones spends in meeting the special needs of each child. Most of the children occupy themselves in painting at the easels, building a U.N. building with blocks, and other individual activities. Miss Jones notices Juan standing near the record player, so she selects his favorite recording. Several days earlier when she played the same aria Juan had said "Opera" hesitantly. Today, on hearing the same music, he questions, "Opera? Opera?" Working from this clue, Miss Jones feels no doubt that the child will profit from the experience of school and that other English words will follow. (They did.)

1:50-2:15 Conversation. All gather about Miss Jones as she tells a story and tries to elicit response in terms of the day's activities.

2:15-2:30 Cleanup and preparation to go home. Only a few of the children need help as they store the equipment they have used and clean up before boarding the bus to go home.

2:30-3:00 Summarizing and recording. Miss Jones jots down the little things she observed during the day that will help her in providing continuity in the program. Juan: "Opera? Opera?" Harold: Took off his sneakers by himself. Jim: Threw the ball again today. He even threw it at Jane.

A DAY WITH TEENAGERS

This class is operated by an Intermediate Unit which crosses school district lines. The children come from seven different school districts to a building with a new wing occupied by five classes of retarded children.

Each child has been in a special class for two or three years, so the parents to some extent expect realistic gains and contribute to their attainment. In a nearby city there is a sheltered workshop, to which the parents are looking for assistance as their teenagers move into a work-study program as part of their school program. Two of the boys will enter a vocational technical school that is operated by the public school system. The parents of one boy will place him in a small residential school because it will be impossible to care for him at home.

The 14 teenagers in the class range in age from 13 years, four months to 15 years, seven months. Most of them learned self-care tasks before the present school year. Two still need to be reminded to brush their teeth at home and three need help in tying shoelaces. Emphasis during the present year is on preparing and serving food for their own group and for two other classes. Most of the group will learn to shop without assistance. (Last year this class learned to prepare and serve their own lunches.) The program is one in which the students have the security of routines and have learned to assume responsibilities in keeping with their abilities.

Sample Schedule

8:30-9:00 Preparation for the day by the teacher, Mr. Brown, who brings anecdotal records up to date in preparation for midterm evaluation of each student. He summarizes records and observations of Tim, whose mother will come at the end of the day for a conference with him. Earlier in the school year Mr. Brown had special days for visiting each home to help him understand each child's home environment.

9:00-9:30 Arrival and plans for the day. The students leave the buses and come to the classroom. Since they are more mature and have been in the program for several years, Mr. Brown does not have to meet the buses. After storing their wraps the pupils congregate at one end of the room to plan for the day, which is a Wednesday. The menus for the week had been planned on Monday and the major shopping completed by the whole class accompanied by the teacher; on Monday, they prepare only their own lunch. Two girls check the supplies and discover that bread and paper napkins are needed, in addition to the meat for the stew they will prepare. Two of the more capable boys, Joe and Don, advise Mr. Brown that it is their turn to go shopping. Then they tell the others how they will shop and where they will find the groceries in the supermarket. After these boys leave, the others examine the menu on the blackboard. Two of them can read the words:

MENU

Stew

Bread and butter

Milk

Chocolate pudding

They talk about what they will need for the stew. Two girls assume responsibility for the cooking of the stew. Others will help. Two boys are put in charge of making the chocolate pudding. One pupil will set the table in this room. The children in the other rooms set their own tables.

9:30-10:00 Gym. After plans for the day are completed and materials assembled, the pupils go outdoors for relays of various kinds with children of another class who are ten, 11, and 12. Two boys play catch at the side of the playground. An immature girl wanders to a primary group and joins in a circle game.

10:00-11:00 Individual projects. The children return to the classroom, where one girl gathers materials needed for sewing an apron. A boy brings out his coat with a missing button and starts to replace the button. Two boys go to the workbench to complete the birdhouse they started several days ago.

11:00-12:15 Preparation of food. Pupils assume responsibility for preparing the foods as planned earlier in the day. Stirring the pudding becomes a chore for the spastic youngster, so Mr. Brown helps him. The more capable members of the class help each other clean carrots and celery and peel potatoes. The only time they need Mr. Brown's assistance is in measuring some of the ingredients. After the food is ready, the meal is carried on trays to the other classes to be served there by the younger children.

12:15-12:45 Lunch. The pupils take their places. Two children serve the food and two others remove dishes at proper times. All are responsible for dishwashing and cleanup.

12:45-1:30 Dishwashing and cleanup. Dishes are washed, dried, and stored by half the class while the others sweep, dust, and put the room in order.

1:30-2:00 Free choice. Some choose table games. One boy plays soft music on the record player. Others look at magazines or indulge in quiet conversation. Mr. Brown gets a rest period at this time by allowing the students to take care of themselves. He checks periodically to make sure no trouble has arisen. One immature child is placed in another room during this period.

2:00-2:30 Folk dancing, square dancing, and ballroom dancing. The group dances in the room next door with children whose teacher has danced professionally.

2:30-2:40 Preparations for leaving.

2:40-3:00 Parent-teacher conference. Mr. Brown discusses with Tim's mother possibilities for helping Tim assume more responsibilities at home. Tim goes to the supermarket by himself at school. (Mr. Brown checks the money spent. Tim cannot count money, but the grocery clerk cooperates in helping Mr. Brown and the children who market.) Tim has learned to ride a public service bus to and from school by himself. He has earned money by cutting lawns in the neighborhood. His parents have become quite realistic in their expectations. Mr. Brown and Tim's mother work together, exploring new ideas for Tim.

8

Observing, Recording, Reporting

The teacher helps the child attain the objectives of an educational program by observing, recording, and reporting as he teaches. The little differences that occur each day provide a continuity that develops and changes as the teacher learns to understand the child. The attentive teacher is attuned to the flutter of an eyelid, indicating perception; to a movement of the hands, feet, or body, reflecting the child's thinking or efforts to socialize; to the initiation of a conversation; to the bit of home the child shyly brings to school. Each teacher learns to observe details and to record them carefully in terms of his own experiences, feelings toward the child, and personal idiosyncracies.

Observing and recording the clues in children's behavior is a vital part of day-by-day planning for each child. The records are used in writing reports to parents, in parent-teacher conferences, in parent education groups, and in helping parents share with the teacher what is happening at home. They are used to plot the growth and development of each child as an individual and in planning for the group.

Some samples of records and reports of teachers and parents are given on the following pages.

NED

Ned is a nine-year-old whose teacher and parents observe and report his growth in various ways.

Excerpts from Teacher's Anecdotal Records

September 10—Ned is quiet and at times withdrawn. Would not eat lunch; wanted to go home. Wanders. No verbal communication.

September 12—Wanders about the room. Would not eat lunch today.

September 18—Brought cookies today and seemed happy to share them with me.

February 5—Today Ned asked for the puppet dance by saying "pup-pet." This was his first attempt to verbalize his desire. Pantomime supported his word.

February 10—Ned is adding simple words to his language daily. He now refers to teacher as "Jones."

February 12—Ned is very helpful about the room and with his classmates, especially Jim and Joe. Single words continue to predominate his verbal efforts.

April 15—Ned came into room with a big smile and said, "Bim?" meaning gym. I said, "Yes, we're going to the gym." He said, "Ball?" I then gave him the ball to take to the gym. While there he enjoyed a game of hiding with another teacher. He counted, in his babbling language, and then he found her. When he found her he laughed heartily and jumped up and down, clapping his hands. He helped Mary set the tables for lunch. Afterwards he swept part of the room. When we went to the lavatory, he called the girls as he pointed to the word "Girls" on the door and said, "Girls, come out," in his way, which I understood. He pointed to Susie's dress and said, "Jones, gess."

Teacher's End-of-Year Summary

Ned had no oral communication in September except for an occasional "Yep" or "No." He depended on pantomime because he could make himself so clearly understood. Now he includes words like "Jones," "John," "Rene," "baby." Two or more words are used on occasion, but one-word expressions are still dominant. He is helpful about getting ready for lunch and cleaning after lunch. He will help sweep, pour out left-over milk, and wash dishes and silver. He likes to bring the large waste basket to empty the baskets from our classroom. He is very kind to the younger children. He takes them by the hand and walks with them and will try to calm them when they are unhappy.

Teacher's Report to Ned's Parents at End of School Year

Dear Parents:

This report includes some new achievements of your son, Ned, between January and June.

Ned has adjusted well in the various classroom activities and his interest span has greatly increased. He wanders away from the group much less frequently and often asks for special activities such as music, catch ball, and bowling.

He is very kind and is always ready to help or appease an upset classmate.

Ned is very sociable and asks to visit the class across the hall.

He enjoys painting and now paints with bold strokes of the brush.

He likes music and often asks for "The Little Puppet." He sometimes sings very loudly.

Ned is beginning to use less and less pantomime and verbalizes with one-word expressions like "girls," "John," "Rene," "Jones," "baby," "gym," "out," "pour," "ball," "bounce," and many others less clearly.

Ned readily takes an active part in all activities and is well liked by his classmates, other children in the school, and the teachers.

End-of-Year Report from Mother to Teacher

In communication and language Ned is doing very well. He is not afraid to try all words and is willing to repeat a few times without being discouraged. He also talks more with strangers with less help of signs in movement.

He loves all children and is terribly hurt when he is rejected. When he plays with smaller children he is very patient, gives in to them and shares prized toys without malice toward children who break them.

He does not let the members of his family get away with

anything. He is cooperative in all things but will not let us tell him how to handle his pets (dog and rooster). He feeds them, trains them, and treats them better than he treats the family. He loves us, but lately we have noticed a strong will of having his own way.

On school days he will do absolutely nothing for himself. Comes Saturday morning, he is up at break of dawn, washes, dresses and feeds himself, and would gladly go out if not stopped. He takes care of himself outdoors, that is, is careful when crossing streets although he is not encouraged to wander away from the neighborhood.

MABEL

Teacher's Early Impressions of Mabel

Last fall I looked at Mabel and shook my head in hopelessness. "What goes on in that head? Does she think any thoughts?" I tried to put myself in Mabel's place—to see things as she did, to try to feel her emotions—but I couldn't.

One day as we waited for the bus, she stood on the outside steps and she moved her head, saying, "Um, um," a monotonous sound that seemingly had no meaning or relation to the situation. We had a long wait and I wondered if she thought, "Where is the bus? I am hungry and thirsty. I'd like to sit down on the bus and go home to Mommy." If not these thoughts, did she have others?

Mother's Report at End of School Year (Excerpts)

I firmly believe school and home are intertwined in Mabel's development. We had a "taking-off-the-shoes" problem here as well as in school. Mrs. Nelson, my husband, and I have told Mabel not to take off her shoes. We no longer have this situation at home and I believe it has been alleviated at school also.

I now have an assistant in "kitchen police" work. Mabel helps set the table, later cleaning it off. Lately, after I have rinsed the dishes and put them into warm, soapy, wash water, Mabel goes to the sink and washes them. Without being told, she uses a scouring pad on the pans and puts the dishes in the dish rack on the counter. She gets very angry if I try to take over. Happily, very few items have to be rewashed.

Mabel's greatest gains have been a new awareness of surroundings, a happier disposition, an ability to carry through a request to do something, and a lessening of tension and frustration. If these general improvements continue, my husband and I firmly believe some speech will come. How much? I guess none of us knows, but we hope Mabel keeps forging ahead a little at a time and retains what she has mastered. We are greatly pleased with her development.

Many other little improvements have taken place, but those I mentioned show, to our minds, the greatest contrast of Mabel "before and after."

JIMMIE

Another teacher reports the progress of Jimmie, a fifteen-year-old.

End-of-Year Report

Before Jimmie came into the group he was a withdrawn, fearful boy who soiled himself at least once a week. He spoke only when spoken to and worked only when told to do so. (He knew he was not wanted.)

When he came into the class in the middle of the semester, he had little initiative. He just sat quietly in his chair, not contributing to the class activities or to the discussions.

After a few weeks he became a definite asset to the group. Full of fun, witty, and humorous, Jimmie gets up and dances to make the children laugh. "I'm a monkey, chee, chee. . . . I'm a mouse, squeek."

Jimmie is a good worker, always ready to be a part of a group activity. In household arts he shows initiative. He is capable of preparing the dessert, coconut pudding, for the whole class, by taking the bowl and egg beater out of the closet, using the correct amount of milk and then mixing the ingredients himself. Jimmie can spread a sandwich and cut it in half. With supervision he sets the table for lunch. He is able to serve the sandwiches to the children and then sit down and eat. After lunch he does a good job of cleaning up. He will clean the tables, help with the dirty dishes by washing and wiping them. He can sweep the floor and set the chairs back where they belong.

In dramatic play about the circus, he says, "I be a monkey; look I scratch myself."

He has not had any real trouble as reported before he came to this class, and is happier for it. He is content with the group and they enjoy being with him.

ROBERT

Another teacher uses a different form for his report in describing seven-year-old Robert's progress.

End-of-Year Report

Social Adjustment:
Robert's greatest achievement has been shown in his attempts to do more things for himself without too much help from an adult. He assumes responsibility in setting up play equipment and putting it away. He enjoys setting up the plastic pins for bowling. He shares toys and takes turns willingly. He has been kicking and fighting some during the past few weeks. When reprimanded, he immediately says, "I'm sorry."

Physical Activity:
Robert enjoys marching, running, sliding, jumping, and tumbling. He can throw and bounce a ball quite well. He walks up and down the stairs independently. He uses a hammer and saw with little help.

Music and Rhythms:
He follows and listens to music, both vocal and instrumental. He sings alone when encouraged and plays with rhythm sticks by keeping time to the music. He responds to

activity games like "In and Out the Window" and spontaneously joins in finger plays.

Self-Care:
Robert seldom needs help in taking off coats and jackets—only occasionally, when a fastener is complicated. He eats neatly and remains seated until he is finished. He cleans up without being reminded and puts away supplies without assistance. He accepts rest period. He knows how to comb his hair. He is able to use a handkerchief when necessary and is alert to help Tim and Joe with a tissue. When he needs to go to the toilet he can be depended upon to make his need known.

Art:
Robert likes to daub with paint, using fingers, spoon, or brush. He draws shapes and usually gives them names, such as "A Boy with a Balloon." He can cut and paste.

Household Arts:
At lunch time Robert sets the table and distributes the milk independently. He can open his jar of food and thermos with little hesitance. He carefully pours the milk with an occasional spilling but quickly cleans this with a sponge. He enjoys washing the dishes with Kenneth, carrying on conversation pertaining to home experience. He sets up his cot and replaces it after rest.

Communication:
Robert's speech is clearer now than at the beginning of the school year. He now communicates in complete sentences. He interprets musical sounds with bodily movements, as in the "Round Wagon." He can sing a song and perform alone if requested, as in the "Marching Song." He imitates actions, as in finger plays with actions. He spontaneously identifies people by name. He uses "big" and "little" in sentences with comprehension. He acts as host with considerable poise. He asks and answers questions. He is attentive while watching movies during visual instruction. He listens to stories and will later interpret them.

VALUE OF COOPERATIVE REPORTING

Preparing conventional report cards, with standardized grading in subjects, is impossible for teachers of these children. Each child presents a unique problem and challenge to the teacher. Any educational program must, of necessity, be a cooperative venture between home and school.

Both teachers and parents may have to search their souls to determine their own feelings for the child. Any subconscious antipathy they harbor may affect the child's progress.

Before the child enters the class, his parents and teacher become acquainted in initial conferences, and the teacher explains the philosophy of the school program. The parents, by observing the class in progress, begin to understand the meaning of the program.

The teacher establishes a relaxed line of communication between school and home by exchanging anecdotes concerning the child's behavior. Group meetings and written reports complete the behavioral record and also the parents' understanding of the program. After conferring with the teacher, parents learn to restrict or amplify home duties and help the child utilize his time to best advantage. In planning summer vacations or camp experiences, parents consider the kind of experiences the child needs at that particular time. For some children social experiences are needed most; for others an environment with little stimulation is essential.

The continual interchange of information between teacher and parents requires that both develop powers of observation and the ability to report observations, to insure a coordinated program for the child. This necessitates time, patience, and effort for all concerned, but it pays dividends in the child's development.

9

Evaluating the School Program

Programs reflect the goals and standards underlying their organization. Child-centered programs based on an education-oriented philosophy have great validity. Expedient baby-sitting programs have no place in an educational setting.

An administrator's personal rejection or acceptance of an educational program will influence the possibilities for its success. The manner in which he approaches the administrative organization of special classes will affect the atmosphere of the entire school.

In activating a program, the community's readiness to accept it is of major importance. Public relations efforts stemming cooperatively from the school and parents are effective. Where administrators are actively interested in parent groups, healthy programs emerge. Where administrators must be pressured into starting a class, there is little likelihood of success.

If a program is to be successful it should have a written policy that includes specification of behavioral objectives and identification of the children served. Physical facilities and transportation must be available. Other requirements include provision for evaluation, integration, reports, records, meetings, conferences, preparation of teachers, parent education, follow-up, and supervision.

The following "Check List for Program Quality" indicates elements essential to a program embodying the greatest possible educational value. Administrators may find the list useful in planning new programs or in evaluating programs already in existence.

CHECK LIST FOR PROGRAM QUALITY

A. The school undertakes the pursuit of behavioral and instructional objectives that grow out of the need of each family unit to find ways and means of establishing and maintaining the normalization of its life cycle. These objectives are achieved by:
1. the school and the home working as an educational team;
2. enabling the child to function in ways considered to be within the norms of his society;
3. giving each individual the opportunity to undergo the normal developmental experiences of his life cycle;
4. taking into consideration and respecting the choices, wishes, and desires of each child;
5. helping shape the attitudes and values of society to be more accepting and tolerant of differentness in appearance, demeanor, intelligence, speech and language, nationality, education, race, color, and ethnic background.

B. The school develops procedures for early identification and referrals which include:
1. work with community agencies (i.e., clinics);
2. criteria for screening children (finding placement for every child);
3. selection (exclusion practices should be eliminated);
4. development of evaluation and dissemination practices.

C. The school makes provision for physical facilities with:
1. sufficient indoor space for movement;
2. sufficient outdoor space for movement;
3. adequate lighting;
4. sufficient wall space;
5. adequate toilet facilities adjoining rooms for young children;

6. adequate toilet facilities nearby for older children;
7. adequate storage space for wraps;
8. adequate storage space for supplies and equipment;
9. open shelves for books and blocks;
10. sink with hot and cold running water in each room;
11. homemaking equipment for older children.

D. The school provides adequate transportation for:
    1. children for whom transportation is feasible;
    2. children within a reasonable distance from the school.

E. The school employs a certificated special education teacher who:
    1. understands child growth and development;
    2. has realistic expectations at all levels of functioning and recognizes that all children have some ability to learn;
    3. meets the needs of children within a particular age range;
    4. uses physical movement in activities (structured and unstructured);
    5. makes good use of music and other arts;
    6. makes skillful use of time;
    7. observes and records behavior of children and uses written reports effectively;
    8. likes children and does not show that he may not like all children equally;
    9. is prepared to distribute affection freely without infantilizing the child or intruding on him;
    10. gives the child guidelines to behavior that are appropriate to his ability level;
    11. maintains a balance between leaving the child free to find his own structure and giving him one to use;
    12. enjoys seeing children in action;
    13. does not readily become involved emotionally with individual children;
    14. communicates on the child's level of understanding;
    15. has physical stamina;
    16. is "human"—may be frustrated on some occasions and maintain a sense of humor on others;

17. has the ability to suppress his own fears and maintain his composure in dealing with unexpected difficulties, objectionable behavior, or upsetting circumstances;
18. is realistic in seeing a child in relation to others;
19. subordinates himself in a child-centered approach;
20. provides sufficient opportunities for parent-teacher interaction;
21. establishes good relationships with co-workers;
22. views his own feelings toward a child realistically;
23. plans and carries out a consistent program that has continuity;
24. does not do for the child those things the child is able to do for himself.

F. The school includes the class as an integral part of the school system by:
1. integrating the class with children of normal intelligence as far as possible, rather than segregating it;
2. giving the teacher the same responsibility and privileges as other members of the faculty;
3. providing the teacher with support and direction from the principal;
4. providing supervision with reinforcement and assistance.

G. The school develops cumulative records which include:
1. results of psychological evaluations;
2. anecdotal records;
3. complete health records;
4. referrals to and from community agencies;
5. family background data;
6. written reports from teachers to parents;
7. written reports from parents to teachers;
8. records of parent-teacher conferences.

H. The school arranges joint meetings of administrators, teachers, psychologists, and social workers, to evaluate:
1. the child's social and emotional status;
2. problems regarding progress;
3. pressures and demands of school, home, and community;

4. plans for experiences in classroom, school, home, and community that will aid in development;
5. plans for moving children into other programs.

I. The school facilitates evaluation of children by:
1. encouraging teachers to make daily anecdotal records;
2. keeping cumulative records up to date;
3. checking cumulative records periodically to see what clues they contain;
4. interpreting effects of socioeconomic levels;
5. learning about emotional climate of home;
6. encouraging written reports to parents;
7. encouraging written reports to teachers from parents;
8. encouraging teachers to visit homes;
9. inviting parents to visit school;
10. showing willingness to learn from parents.

J. The school arranges periodic conferences (weekly, in beginning stages) with parents of children to:
1. review their progress;
2. consider their needs in home, school, and community;
3. encourage parental cooperation in school activities which affect their welfare;
4. explore possibilities for sharing with and learning from parents;
5. build a 24-hour-a-day schedule between each home and the school that contains experiences geared to the normalization of the life cycle of the family.

K. Provision is made for meeting the special needs of children by:
1. teachers;
2. administrators and supervisors;
3. psychologists;
4. physicians;
5. nurses;
6. social workers;
7. physical therapists;
8. parents.

L. Provision is made for use of community resources in developing programs by:
1. surveys of community resources;
2. supervised excursions;
3. help from parents and community agencies.

M. Provision is made to participate in activities with other children:
1. in the classroom;
2. in physical education classes;
3. on the playground;
4. in the cafeteria;
5. in assemblies.

N. The school provides in-service training by:
1. meetings of special education teachers with each other;
2. meetings of special education teachers with teachers of other children;
3. workshops and study groups;
4. participation in conferences and conventions;
5. use of outside consultants;
6. flexible approach to identification procedures and their interpretation;
7. visits of teachers to other classes and schools;
8. study of methods of observation, recording, and reporting;
9. study of methods of charting progress of each child;
10. openness to new ideas in instructional materials and classroom procedure;
11. openness to new ideas in administrative arrangements;
12. assistance in curriculum construction.

O. The school interprets the program to:
1. faculty members;
2. the general public;
3. other educators;
4. related professions;
5. community agencies.

P. The school includes programs in parent education by:
1. involving parents as integral parts of the planning and execution of programs;
2. providing the assistance of administrators, teachers, a psychologist, therapists, and a social worker in meetings and conferences;
3. including parents in the regular P.T.A.

Q. The school explores possibilities for the child as he leaves the elementary school in:
1. the secondary school;
2. a sheltered environment outside the home, if needed.

R. The school follows up children who leave school to go to:
1. homes;
2. residential schools;
3. other environments.

CONCLUSION

The child enters an educational program as a total entity combining biology, environment, and experiences. As he learns to express himself and communicate with others, he gains awareness of who he is and what he can do. He learns acceptable patterns of social and personal behavior and useful family living and work skills.

The teacher draws upon the knowledge provided by the physician, the psychologist, the social worker, and the parents. Observations, records, and reports provide the backbone for interaction, assessment and intervention, evaluation, and dissemination.

The ultimate success or failure of an educational program for these children will be determined by the administrator, the supervisor, the teacher, and the community, by virtue of their readiness to accept the program and the standards underlying it. Every child can grow and learn if he is helped and expected to do so.

Appendices

The forms included in this Appendix are used to help people educate children with handicapping conditions. These materials have been used as in-service tools at the local level in many states. They are included here to help college instructors, supervisors, teachers, teacher aides, and parents develop an ongoing process of change, as described throughout this book. No doubt readers will think of other ideas appropriate to their own situations.

Assessment and Intervention

This form is used to help teachers learn to observe and plan for each child with realistic diagnostic and prescriptive procedures, emphasizing the success of each child as a starting point.

Evaluating Prescriptive Teaching

Supervisors, administrators, and college instructors use this form to help teachers evaluate their own teaching.

The Learning Situation

This form is used by teachers to help them provide the diagnostic and prescriptive teaching meaningful to the individual child within a group situation. It can be used to replace the traditional lesson plan.

Case Study

This skeleton case study is used as practice for teachers, parents, and professionals from related disciplines in the development of prescriptive teaching to meet individual needs. For instance, groups of people may be asked to tell how they would meet the needs of this child. Shared group findings are disseminated among the various individuals involved. Later, teachers prepare similar skeleton case studies with this form as models. Parents and professionals alike are often amazed to discover the rich resources at their fingertips when they begin to seek them. The resulting interaction helps eliminate unfounded fear and apprehension in working with low-functioning children. Teachers and others can begin to use the information they obtain from such interaction in developing guidelines for their curriculum at the local level.

Matching Materials to Children

This sample form is used by teachers in matching materials to the developmental needs of each child. As teachers observe the unique needs of each child they become proficient in locating suitable materials. Supervisors collect, reproduce, and compile numbers of such forms and disseminate them as needed.

APPENDIX A:

ASSESSMENT AND INTERVENTION

Name _____ Date _____

Chronological Age _____

Location _____ Recorder_____

Where does this child achieve success?

What works?
How do you get his attention?
How do you set limits for him to achieve by himself?
For him to achieve in a group?

How does he learn?

What sensory input seems most effective? In what situations?

What reinforcement is needed? (continuing analysis)

What motivates him to complete a task?

What is his design for growth and development?

What skills has he mastered in each area? (Identify broad areas, then specific skills.)

What skills should he acquire at the next step higher?

How will you provide learning situations designed to develop the next skills?

For this individual by himself?

For this individual in group situations?

When should learning situations be planned to develop certain skills? (Specify skills.)

At what hours of day?

On what days of week?

At what time of year?

Length of time, e.g., 10 minutes per day? Hourly? Throughout his life?

How will you know when it is time to move to the next higher step? In nurturing skills? In providing reinforcements?

How will you provide for continuous evaluation?

How do you plan to disseminate information concerning your intervention with personnel in other disciplines?

How do you learn from others involved (parents, teachers, teacher aides)?

APPENDIX B:

EVALUATING PRESCRIPTIVE TEACHING

1. Does the teacher know where the pupil achieves success?
2. Does the teacher know what works for each individual—how to get and hold his attention?
3. Does the teacher know how each one learns?
   Is this evident in his teaching? How?
4. Does motivation grow out of the child's needs?
5. Are the children "alive"? Bored?
6. Does the teacher do too much talking?
7. Does the teacher reach each individual?
8. Is the lesson important? To whom?
9. Are the child's changing growth patterns the basis for planning?
10. Does the teacher get to the child's level—chronological and social?
11. Do the pupils understand what they are to do next?
12. Does the teacher sequence activities to the pupil's functioning level and in keeping with ability to perform?
13. What observations are recorded by the teacher?
14. How do the observations relate to the expanding plans for each child?
    How do they relate to the evaluation of the teacher?
15. Does the classroom or living area reflect current learning?
16. Are comprehensive weekly lesson plans (including individualized plans) available each Friday for the following week?
17. Are plans for individual prescriptive teaching developed within the 24-hour day for each?
    Are plans fragmented?
18. Does the teacher coordinate plans with those of other personnel—with physical education, physical therapy, speech and hearing, social work, and psychology? How?
19. Can you "feel" a healthy emotional climate as you enter the room?
    Is there a sense of fear? Of rigidity?

20. Does the program have a balance between active and quiet experiences?
21. Is subject matter adequate to meet the needs of every child in the group?
22. Does the teacher provide adequate concrete instructional materials for developmental sequencing?
23. Are cumulative records kept up to date?
    Are sufficient samplings of each pupil's work that show behavior changes included in the cumulative folder?
24. How are parents involved in the give and take of programming?
25. Is the evaluation of each pupil's progress comprehensive and consistent? Explain.

APPENDIX C:

THE LEARNING SITUATION

1. Why did the teacher use the situation (i.e., its objectives)?
2. In what area is the situation planned (language arts, art, number concepts, physical education, etc.)?
3. How does the situation relate to activities during other parts of the day?
4. What time of day can the situation be used?
5. Responsibility for activity
6. Preparation of instructional materials
7. Preparation of room
8. Sequencing: what comes next?
9. Outcome—Evaluation
   Need for change in planning
   Gains
10. Recommended follow-up procedures

APPENDIX D:

CASE STUDY

Jim

Jim has a chronological age of five years. (If this case study is used with teachers working with older children, the chronological age may be changed accordingly.)

Physical Development

General physical condition: fair
Not on medication
Epileptic: has periodic seizures (lies on floor)
Nonambulatory, no use of right arm or leg
Cerebral palsied
Hears gross sounds
Pushes objects close to eyes to see them

Social Communication

Uses movements and gestures to denote needs
Makes sounds to get attention

Motor and Perceptual Development

Gross Motor
   Raises head
   Moves left hand and foot
   Sits with aid
Fine Motor
   Extends fingers of left hand
   Grasps objects (poor grasp)
Visual-Motor
   Attends to visual stimuli
   Eyes follow moving object
Auditory
   Responds with startle to loud noise
   Turns head to auditory stimuli
   Changes activity with change of sound

Tactile-Kinesthetic
>   Touches objects with left hand and left foot
>   Pushes large objects

Self-Concept

>   Appears tense
>   Screams when approached by stranger

Self-Care

>   Not completely toilet trained (mother places him on toilet at what appears to be right time)
>   Does not feed self; pushes cracker or cookie to mouth

Social Interaction

>   Plays alone

Parents' Comments

>   Negative

Success?

APPENDIX E:

MATCHING MATERIALS TO CHILDREN

1. *Name of material:* ladies' purse, wallet, key ring with keys.
2. *Description of material:* purse had zippers and clasps; wallet had snaps and many sections; key ring had several keys.
3. *How was this material used to meet behavioral goals?*
   In general (for a class). All children used the purse; some only to see what was inside, others to manipulate the various parts.
   For a specific child. A specific child was introduced to it because it being a familiar object he could accept it more readily. The child was at the crawling stage but would not stop to see or observe what was around him.

Where was the child? In class, on the floor.

How was material adapted to child's needs? The purse was placed near the child. Its familiar appearance (it was his mother's) called it to his attention. He began to look at it, touch it, and finally to manipulate it to learn what is was all about. It was the only object that would hold his attention. It provided him with an opportunity to observe an object, learn to manipulate and develop some hand skills. It gave him a basis for moving on to other objects and toys.

Selected References

1. Andrews, Gladys, Saurborn, Jeanette, and Schneider, Elsa. *Physical Education for Today's Boys and Girls.* Boston: Allyn and Bacon, 1960.
   This is a book about movement. It points out the importance of movement as the foundation of physical education, as well as the social conditions that affect the physical activity opportunities of children. It describes in detail the various forms of movement that should be included in a physical education program.
2. Arin Intermediate Unit. *A Motor-Academic-Perceptual Curriculum Guide for the Early Education of the Multiply-Handicapped.* Indiana, Pa.: Arin Intermediate Unit #28, 1973.
   This program is designed to develop, through research and experimentation, a practical, sequentially developed, motor/academic/perceptual curriculum for the early childhood education of the handicapped.
3. Auerbach, Aline B. *Parents Learn through Discusssion, Principles and Practices of Parent Group Education.* New York: Wiley, 1968.
   This material grows out of the premise that "the primary approach to the healthy development of children and the prevention of deviant development is best accomplished in assisting parents."

4. Baumgartner, Bernice B. and Lynch, Katherine D. *Administering Classes for the Retarded, What Kinds of Principals and Supervisors are Needed?* New York: John Day, 1968.
   This is a book for administrators, supervisors, and others responsible for the mentally retarded.
5. Baumgartner, Bernice B. and Shultz, Joyce B. *Reaching Children through Art.* Johnstown, Pa: Mafex Associates, 1969.
   The emphasis in this book is on the process the teacher uses in helping the child with special needs express himself through art. Included are chapters on the philosophy of learning through art, a healthy classroom climate, and art curriculum, with charts to be used in teaching and in evaluation.
6. Becker, Wesley C. *Parents Are Teachers, A Child Management Program.* Champaign, Ill.: Research Press, 1971.
   This book is designed to help parents learn to be more effective teachers of their children.
7. Bensberg, Gerald J. *Teaching the Mentally Retarded.* Atlanta: Southern Regional Education Board, 1965.
   This book presents principles and methods for teaching the young and severely retarded.
8. Bzoch, Kenneth R. and League, Richard. *Assessing Language Skills in Infancy.* Gainesville, Fla.: Tree of Life Press, 1971.
   This handbook is useful in the multi-dimensional analysis of emergent language.
9. Connor, Frances P. and Talbot, Mabel E. *An Experimental Curriculum for Young Mentally Retarded Children.* New York: Teachers College Press, 1964.
   This experimental curriculum is a description of a special education program for preschool educable mentally retarded children. It is especially valuable in developing levels of functioning and in providing the know-how for prescriptive teaching.
10. Frailburg, Selma M. *The Magic Years.* New York: Scribner, 1959.
   The "magic years" are the years of early childhood.

This book tells the story of personality development during the first years of life and describes and discusses some of the typical problems that emerge at each developmental stage.

11. Haeusserman, Elsa. *Developmental Potential of Pre-School Children.* New York: Greene and Stratton, 1958.

Miss Haeusserman's approach is helpful in building realistic prescriptive teaching. Emphasis is on description and interpretation of the child's capacities and performance to provide a solid basis for growth and/or rehabilitation.

12. Heber, Rick, Garber, Howard, Harrington, Susan, Hoffman, Caroline, and Falender, Carol. "Rehabilitation of Families at Risk for Mental Retardation." Madison, Wis.: University of Wisconsin, 1972.

This is a progress report of a longitudinal study designed to determine whether "cultural-familial" or "sociocultural" mental retardation can be prevented through a program of family intervention beginning in early infancy.

13. Hunt, Nigel. *The World of Nigel Hunt.* New York: Garret, 1967.

This autobiography was written by a young adult who has Down's syndrome. It is a view of the inner reflections of the young man in which he reviews some of his travels with his parents. The book documents what some adults with Down's syndrome can attain with attention, education, and parental involvement when expectations are realistic.

14. Hymes, James L. Jr. *A Child Development Point of View.* Englewood Cliffs, N.J.: Prentice-Hall, 1965.

The work teachers do in building strengths, in building good feelings into children is the point of departure in prevention and in mental health.

15. ——. *Teaching the Child Under Six.* Columbus, O.: Merrill, 1968.

Dr. Hymes has built into this book two of his hopes: (1) that the day will come when all young children begin school at three and (2) that we serve young children well.

16. Jersild, Arthur T. *When Teachers Face Themselves.* New York: Teachers College Press, 1955.

Discussion centers on the teacher, whose "understanding and acceptance of himself is the most important requirement in any effort he makes to help students know themselves and to gain healthy attitudes of self-acceptance."

17. Karnes, Merle B. *Helping Young Children Develop Language Skills: A Book of Activities.* Washington, D.C.: The Council for Exceptional Children, 1968.

Although these activities were developed for use with small groups of young disadvantaged children, they can be used with mentally retarded children in need of such skills at any age.

18. Lippman, Leopold and Goldberg, I. Ignacy. *Right to Education.* New York: Teachers College Press, 1973.

This is subtitled *Anatomy of the Pennsylvania Case and Its Implications for Exceptional Children.* The authors describe what they see as the characteristics of the development of the mental retardation movement. "The significance of this report is seen in . . . its thorough and painstaking research into the genesis, the origin of this milestone case and . . . its insight in drawing implications for further development of programs for the handicapped."

19. Mager, Robert F. *Preparing Instructional Objectives.* Belmont, Cal.: Fearon, 1962.

This book is of value for those involved in pinpointing behavioral objectives.

20. *Physical Activities for the Mentally Retarded.* Washington, D.C.: American Association for Health, Physical Education and Recreation, 1968.

This manual of guidelines is useful in planning individualized programs.

21. Pitcher, Evelyn G. and Ames, Louise B. *The Guidance Nursery School.* New York: Harper and Row, 1964.

Helping teachers and parents appreciate the complexity and immaturity of a child is vital in early stages of education. This book presents steps by which skilled, sympathetic, and understanding teachers and/or parents can guide the child to increasingly higher levels of maturity.

22. *Resource Guide in Sex Education for the Mentally Retarded.* Washington, D.C.: American Association for Health, Physical Education and Recreation, 1971. A developmental approach is used in this guide, with concepts and materials presented sequentially from the basic and easy to more difficult and sophisticated learnings in sex education.

23. *Right to Education, Compile.* Harrisburg, Pa.: Right to Education Office, 1972.
This material was developed as a result of a Federal Court order resulting from a class action suit brought by the Pennsylvania Association for Retarded Children against the Commonwealth of Pennsylvania, its representatives, and various school boards. The order indicates that all school-aged children must be educated by the public schools regardless of the degree of handicap.

24. Stephens, Beth. *Training the Developmentally Young.* New York: John Day, 1971.
This group collaboration evolved from an attempt to devise an outline for a university course whose goal was to prepare teachers to work with the moderately retarded.

25. Stull, C. Edward. "Southbury Classification Plan," *American Journal of Mental Deficiency*, LXIII (May, 1959), 1022-1029.

26. Valett, Robert E. *The Remediation of Learning Disabilities: A Handbook of Psycho-Educational Resource Programs.* Belmont: Cal.: Fearon, 1967.
This publication illustrates approaches for areas such as gross-motor development, sensory-motor integration, perceptual-motor skills, language development, conceptual skills, and social skills.

27. Wright, Betty Atwell. *Teacher Aides to the Rescue.* New York: John Day, 1969.

Practical ideas are related to teacher aide contributions in this book. Included are the kinds of help provided by teacher aides with innovative programs, programs planned to solve problems, and in-service training resources available for teacher aides.

28. Young, Milton A. *Teaching Children with Special Learning Needs.* New York: John Day, 1967.

The author's purposes in writing this book include: emphasizing the individual differences between children; encouraging problem-solving or diagnostic teaching; and giving concrete assistance to those who teach children with learning difficulties.

Children's Bureau Pamphlets, U.S. Government Printing Office, Washington, D.C.:

"The Care of Your Child's Teeth"
"The Child with Cerebral Palsy"
"The Child with a Cleft Palate"
"The Child with Epilepsy"
"The Mentally Retarded Child at Home"
"The Mongoloid Baby"
"Your Preschool Child's Eyes"

Public Affairs Pamphlets, 381 Park Avenue South, New York:

"Cerebral Palsy—More Hope than Ever"
"Epilepsy—Today's Encouraging Outlook"
"How to Discipline your Child"
"Parents' Guide to Children's Vision"
"What Should Parents Expect from Children"
"Your Child's Emotional Health"